The Fencing Book

A COMPREHENSIVE MANUAL
FOR DEVELOPING FENCING SKILLS
AND FUNDAMENTALS

Nancy L. Curry, Ph.D.

A publication of
Leisure Press.
597 Fifth Avenue, New York, N.Y. 10017
Copyright © 1984 Leisure Press
All rights reserved. Printed in the U.S.A.

No part of this publication may be reproduced
or transmitted in any form or by any means
electronic or mechanical, including photocopying, recording,
or any information storage and retrieval system now known
or to be invented, without permission in writing from the publisher,
except by a reviewer who wishes to quote brief passages
in connection with a written review for
inclusion in a magazine, newspaper, or broadcast.

Library of Congress Catalog Card Number: 82-83919

ISBN: 0-918438-99-3

Cover and book design: Catherine Elke Conner
Oakland, California

Acknowledgments

I wish to express my sincere appreciation to the following individuals for their assistance in this work: Mr. Kent Morris, Mr. Mark Sims, and Dr. George Simpson who posed for the photographs; Mr. Jim Salyer and Mr. Robert Arends who served as photographers; The American Fencing Supply Co. of San Francisco who provided the equipment and uniforms; Mrs. Jane Mashburn and Ms. Betty Hindman who typed the manuscript; Dr. Mildred Evans and Mrs. J.E. Hindman who proofed this manuscript.

Foreword

Through the centuries the sword has endured as a badge of authority and honor. Historically, the sword has played an important part in the coronation of royalty. To this date, English monarchs are invested with the sword during an impressive exhortation.

Too little has been written about the "Ancient Art" of fencing with its centuries old tradition. Treatises on fencing have been quite limited for a sport that has an existence of over five hundred years. Dr. Curry's treatise conveys her love for the art of fencing in simple and intelligent terms and may serve as a textbook for the fencer who wishes to increase their knowledge of the sport. The rules for competition should also be exceedingly helpful. Thus, the book is an interesting addition to literary works on fencing and has a place in the annals of the sport.

For close to two decades, I've had the privilege of watching a talented young fencer from the mid-west dedicate herself to popularizing the sport of fencing. Dr. Nancy Curry, a former Iowa State Champion, capitalized on every opportunity to expand her knowledge and skill in fencing. She was an outstanding participant at the 2nd National Institute in Girl's Sports, at Michigan State University in 1965, a workshop held under the auspices of the Olympic Committee.

Dr. Curry, as an Instructor of Physical Education at Iowa State University, organized an accelerated course in fencing at the graduate level in 1966 and her enthusiasm for the sport has never diminished. Presently, as a Professor of Physical Education at Southwest Missouri University in Springfield, Missouri, Dr. Curry teaches fencing and performs in many capacities to promote fencing in the mid-west.

Louis XIV was known to give many privileges and honors to fencing masters. Those with a satisfactory record of at least twenty years were awarded titles and became noblemen. Perhaps Nancy Curry would have been so honored.

I'm impelled to repeat a personal quote, "Today, you don't have to be royalty to flourish a sword. En Garde!"

Julia Jones-Pugliese
Hunter College, CUNY
New York, New York

Contents

I. History   1
- Fencing—What is it? • Past • Present
- Evaluation Questions

II. Equipment   5
- The Sabre • The Epée • The Foil
- The Dress • Electrical Equipment
- Evaluation Questions

III. Basic Skills and Mobility   11
- Grip • Attention • Salute
- Guard Position • Mobility
- Evaluation Questions

IV. Blade Actions   31
- Lines for Action • Engagement
- Target Area • Right of Way • Simple Attack
- Compound Attacks • Attacks Taking the Blade
- Advanced Techniques • Defensive Blade Action
- The Riposte • Counter Attacks
- Evaluation Questions

V. Rules of Play   87
- Condensed A.F.L.A. Rules • Scoring
- Timing • Evaluation Questions

VI. Etiquette and Safety   111
- Courtesy and Tradition • Conduct of Fencers
- Evaluation Questions

VII. Bouting Strategy   115
- Beginning the Bout • Knowing the Opponent
- Strategy for the Left-Handed Fencer
- Evaluation Questions

VIII. Conditioning   121
- Components • The Warm-up
- Free Exercises • Exercise with Weight Machines
- Evaluation Questions

IX. Terminology   137

Suggested Readings   147

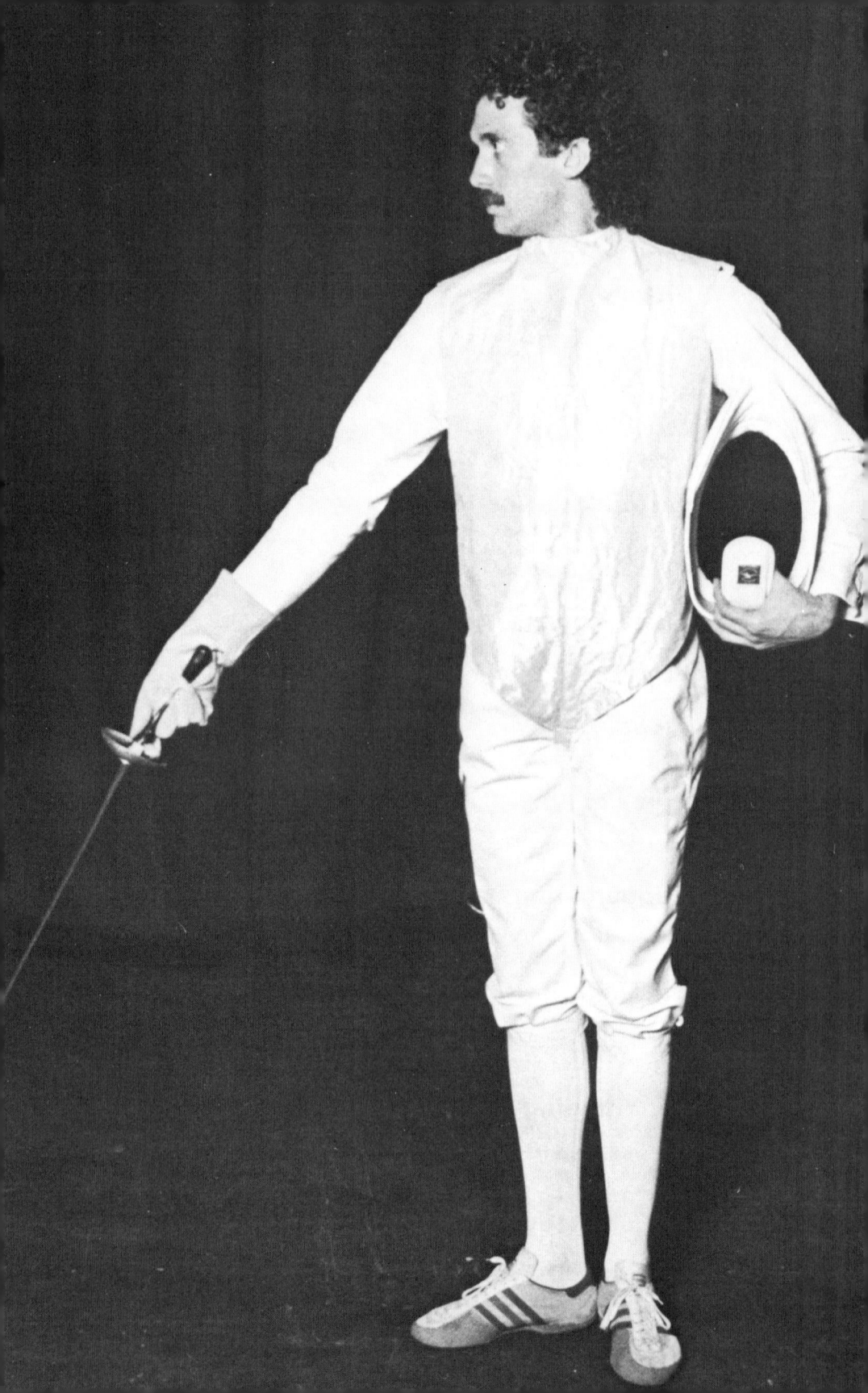

CHAPTER ONE

History

Fencing, the art of offense and defense with a sword, is experiencing a renaissance today. It is a sport that requires the utmost in physical and mental agility.

> *Fencing is the art of giving cuts without receiving them. The necessity of touching the opponent by avoiding his cuts makes the art of fencing very difficult and complicated. The eyes that observe and prevent, the brain that considers and decides, the hand that carries the decision through must harmonize accuracy and speed to give the necessary life to the sword.*[1]

Past

Fencing, one of the most deadly forms of combat, has been traced back beyond the Christian era. Some historians estimate it is more than three thousand years old. With the introduction of firearms at the Battle of Crecy in 1346, the value of the sword as a weapon of war began to depreciate.

The sword, after the advent of firearms, was utilized primarily as a method of settling affairs of honor. These were duels to the death. A gentleman never knew when he might be challenged. Thus, as a safety precaution, the nobility spent considerable time and money learning the art of the sword.

The Germans, during the fourteenth century, felt that the thrill and challenge of dueling could be carried on without the bloodletting. As a result, they began a movement to develop fencing as a sport. They devised blunted practice weapons with which to duel each other, and were the first to utilize an official to supervise the contests. The official would observe the men in a dueling situation for an allotted period of time, at the end of which he would declare the champion. The contest was then considered closed.

Fencing as practiced by the Germans was not readily adopted by other countries where dueling still prevailed. But by the sixteenth century many of the reigning monarchs had become distraught over the great number of courtiers eliminated in duels. In an effort to stop the loss, dueling

---

[1] Julius Palffy-Alpar, *Sword and Masque* (Philadelphia: F.A. Davis Company, 1967), p. 1.

was forbidden altogether and made a criminal offense. This, however, did not put an end to swordplay. Men met at night and in out-of-the-way places to settle their contentions of honor. In fact, it became a mark of courage for a man to duel outside the law.

The German concept of fencing as a sport became increasingly widespread during the fifteenth and sixteenth centuries; however, there was little uniformity in the manner in which the sport was conducted. The weapons were heavier than the ones in modern use. Some of them were made of bronze, some of iron. The English used a sword with a broad blade suitable for cutting, but not for thrusting. The Italians perfected the rapier, a long, straight, two-edged sword with a narrow, pointed blade. The Germans quickly adopted the lightning-quick rapier in place of their traditional heavy, double-edged sword. Frenchmen used still another type of weapon, a short sword similar to the dagger in shape, but somewhat longer. The Spanish used all of the above weapons interchangeably, the choice depending upon their specific needs at the time of the duel.

Although dueling was still commonplace, fencing gained respect as a sport. Fencing masters, who had in the past secretly guarded their sword techniques, began to organize schools. They also began to write books on sword-fighting techniques, thus exposing the sport to an ever-widening audience, and giving it an air of legitimacy.

The most prominent schools of fencing were those developed by the French, Italians, and Spanish. The French school was built on the concept of finesse with the blade, while the premise of the Italian school was to use strength with the blade. The Spanish made an effort to combine the French and Italian schools and utilized a more scientific approach to combat. The sport in the United States today is an admixture of techniques from all three schools.

Fencing began to appear in the United States in the eighteenth century. As the interest grew, many American schools added fencing to their curricula. In 1891 the Amateur Fencers League of America (AFLA) was formed.

Present

The United States Fencing Association (formerly the AFLA) works under the direct auspices of the Fédération d'Escrime (FIE), which is the international fencing organization. The FIE and the USFA and its interested members are the major driving forces behind the continual advancement of fencing as a sport today. These organizations make instructional material available, present clinics, and qualify competitors for all international contests including the Olympic Games. The USFA publishes a

I. HISTORY

manual containing the rules for foil, épée, and sabre fencing.[2] Once an individual has learned the basic movements of fencing, there awaits the life-long challenge of the sword. Many cities have established clubs where one can continue to fence as a lifetime sport. State and local USFA organizations sponsor competition for their members. The initial cost for equipment need only be a few dollars; but a serious student will find that expenses mount quickly. The equipment, if properly cared for, will last many years, although blades will break and must occasionally be replaced.

Fencing is a sport that offers vigorous, but not exhausting, exercise. The rapidity with which a participant must determine offensive and defensive maneuvers makes it an excellent mental activity. Regular participation in fencing can increase cardiovascular, cardiorespiratory, and muscular endurance and can contribute to the development of balance, grace, poise, and coordination.

Evaluation Questions

1. What had the greatest effect on reducing the importance of the sword as a weapon of war?
2. Which nation first attempted to develop fencing as a sport?
3. When did fencing appear in the United States?
4. What is the USFA?
5. What is the name of the world fencing association?

---

[2]United States Fencing Association, 1750 E. Boulder Street, Colorado Springs, CO 80909.

THE FENCING BOOK

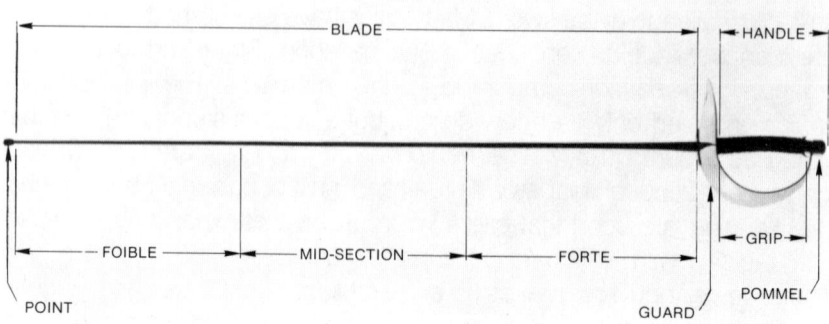

2.1 Sabre

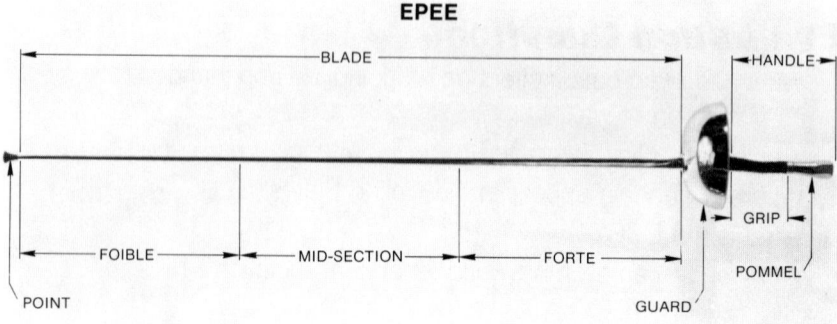

2.2 Epée

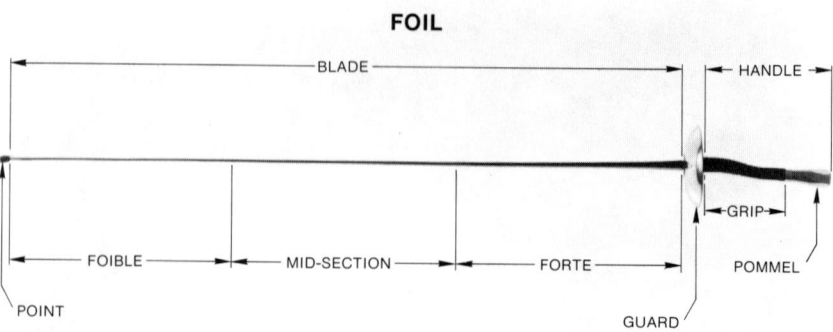

2.3 Foil

CHAPTER TWO

Equipment

The three weapons used in the sport of fencing are the *sabre, épée,* and *foil.* The sabre is used for both cutting and thrusting, while the épée and foil are used only for thrusting. Both men and women compete with all three weapons, but women do not compete against men in tournament play.

The Sabre

The blade of the sabre is rectangular at the forte and tapers to a triangular shape near the foible (*Fig. 2.1*). The thin edge of the foible is used as a cutting edge. The thicker edge is used for parries and attacks on the blade. The target for sabre fencing consists of the torso from the waist up, arms, and head. Cuts or thrusts may be delivered on both the front and the back of the opponent.

The Epée

The blade of the épée is triangular and tapers from the forte to the blunted tip (*Fig. 2.2*). The épée or dueling sword, as it is sometimes called, is much heavier than the foil. The target consists of the entire body. Since the épée is a thrusting weapon, all scores or touches must be made with the point on target.

The Foil

The foil is the lightest of the three weapons (*Fig. 2.3*). The blade is rectangular and tapers from the forte through the flexible foible to the blunted tip. The target for foil fencing includes all the front torso and the back torso down to the waistline. The remainder of the fencer's body, and all the equipment, are considered off-target. The foil is a thrusting weapon; therefore, all valid scores or touches must land with the point in the target area.

The foil, the weapon to which this book is devoted, is considered the basic weapon of the three. Many fencers desire to master the skill and techniques of the foil prior to moving to the épée and sabre. This is not to

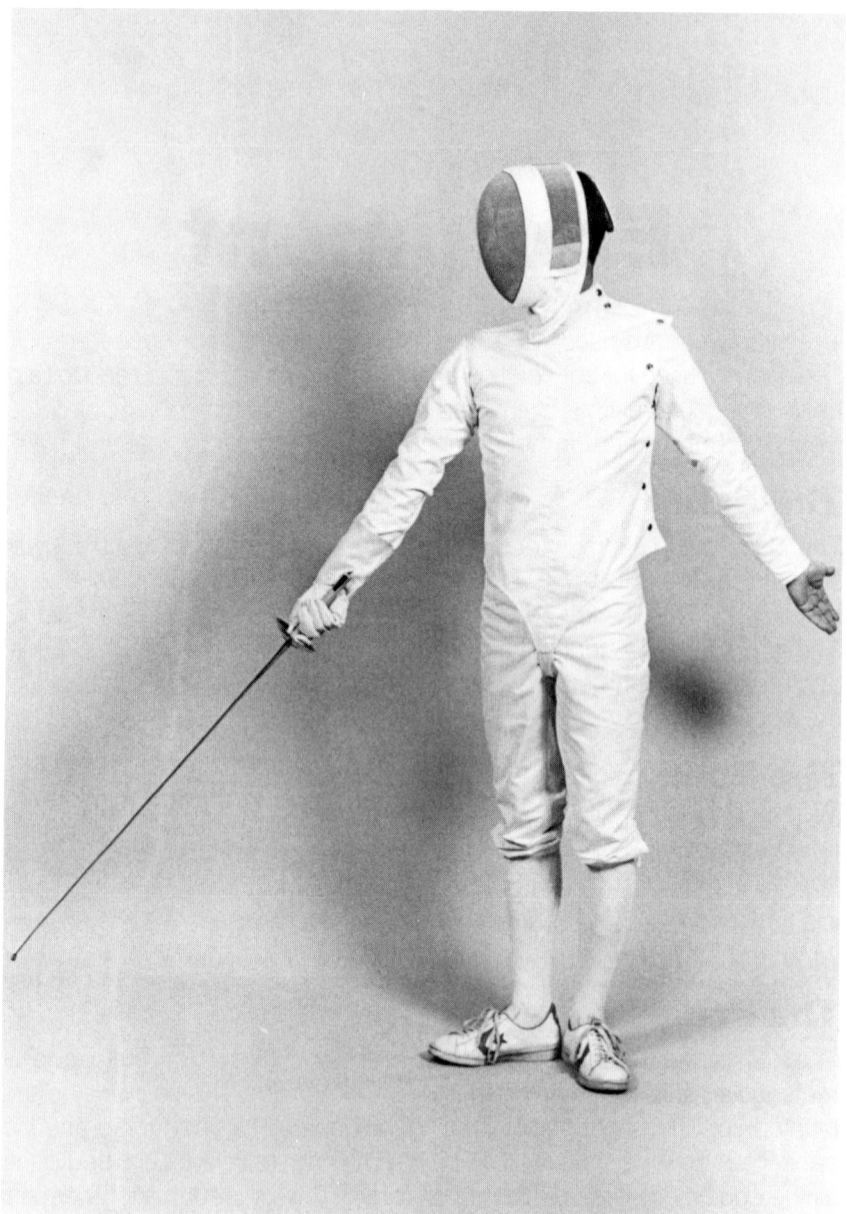

2.4 Proper Dress

say the foil is a beginner's weapon, to be discarded once the techniques are acquired. In fact, it is perhaps the most difficult of the three with which to become truly proficient.

The Dress

Proper fencing dress is mandatory for anyone entering into competition (*Fig. 2.4*). This should be extended into the instructional situation in schools and colleges to insure maximum safety for all participants. (See the rules for a thorough explanation.)

Jacket. The jacket, made of heavy cotton, should be full length to afford maximum protection to the entire target area and to the arms. Although most jackets have a padded lining, women must have additional protection for the breast area. This may be obtained by wearing a quilted plastron, vest, and breast plate under the regulation jacket.

Glove. The glove, or gauntlet, made of leather or canvas, is worn on the foil hand. The outside is padded for hand protection. The sleeve of the jacket should always be tucked inside the gauntlet as a safety precaution, to prevent the opponent's blade from sliding up the sleeve.

Mask. The mask protects the head and is worn at all times when facing an opponent. The front of the mask has a wire mesh covering that protects the face without unduly restricting vision. The tongue, which fits over the top and the back of the head, is the means by which the mask can be adjusted to fit different head sizes and shapes. At the base of the wire mesh is a bib, usually of quilted cotton or plastic, used to protect the fencer's throat. The bib, which normally extends down over the collar of the jacket, is considered off-target.

The official dress of a competitive fencer is all white. Full length trousers or knickers and knee hose are generally worn along with white, rubber-soled shoes. Each item of the aforementioned equipment is necessary to insure the safety of the fencer.

Electrical Equipment

For competition utilizing electrical apparatus, the fencer must wear a body cord under the regulation jacket and use an electrical foil. Over the regulation jacket the fencer must wear a metallic vest. This vest covers all valid target areas (*Fig. 2.5*). For a more thorough discussion, see the chapter on Rules of Play.

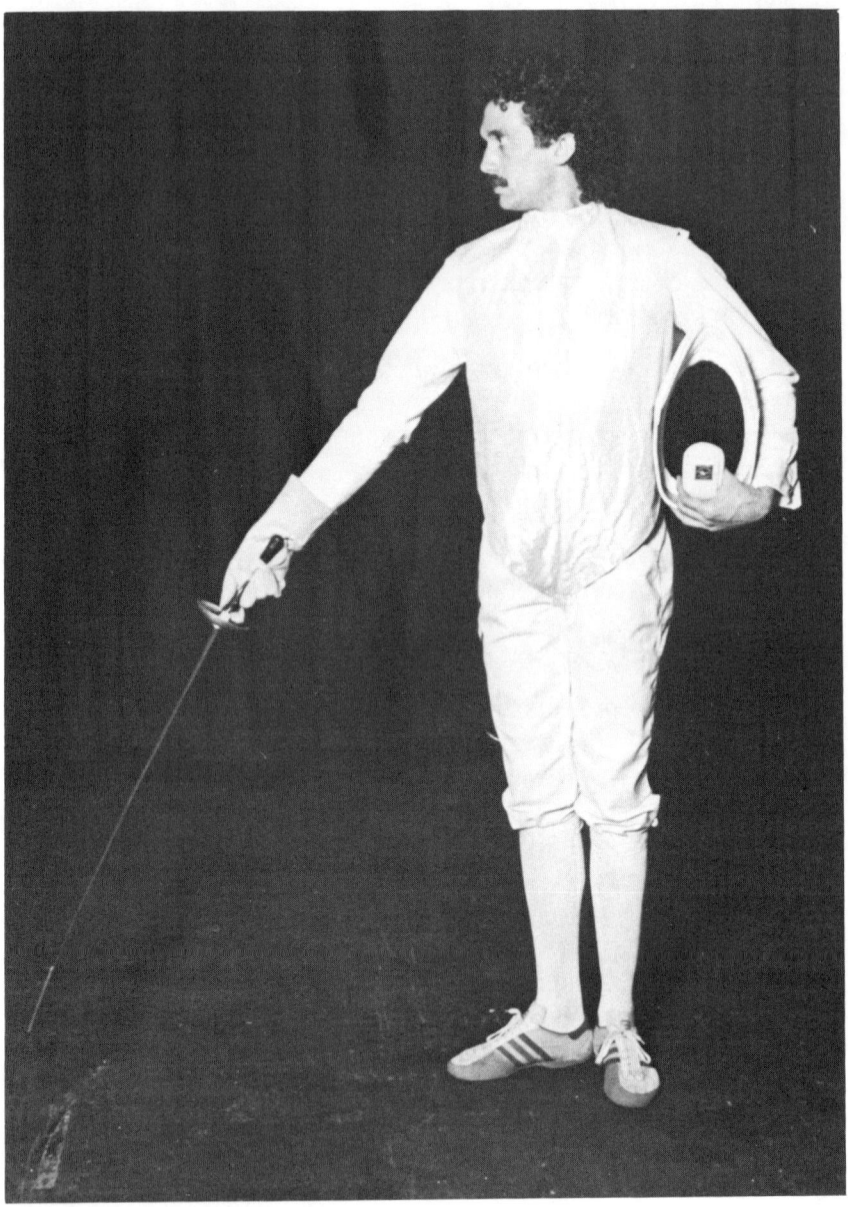

2.5 Electrical Dress

II. EQUIPMENT

Evaluation Questions

1. *What are the three weapons used in the sport of fencing?*
2. *What is the color of dress worn by fencing competitors?*
3. *Is it necessary to wear all items of equipment and dress while fencing?*
4. *Why should the sleeve on one's foil arm be tucked inside the gauntlet?*
5. *Is a metallic vest mandatory for electrical foil competition?*

CHAPTER THREE

Basic Skills and Mobility

For the beginning fencer, it is recommended that a foil with a French grip be utilized in the instructional program (*Fig. 2.3*). This style of grip enables a novice fencer to develop the necessary dexterity and finesse in the use of the blade.

The French grip is proportioned so its convex curve lies diagonally across the palm of the foil hand (*Fig. 3.1*). The upper portion of the grip just below the bell cushion is placed on the second articulation of the index finger. The thumb is then placed on top of the grip and in line with the grip (*Fig. 3.2*). The upper portion of the grip is held primarily between the thumb and the second articulation of the index finger. The primary purpose of the thumb and the index finger is control and accuracy of the blade. They serve as the manipulators of the foil and control the direction and accuracy of the point. The remaining three fingers are angled down the concave side of the grip (*Fig. 3.3*). Their primary function is to serve as the fulcrum during blade action. The grip needs to be sufficiently secure so one is not disarmed by a strong blade action of an opponent. An extremely tight grip should be avoided. This causes undue muscular fatigue in the foil hand and arm, which can move upward through the shoulder girdle. An excellent analogy has been given for the proper control of the foil by the foil hand and arm. Imagine one is holding a small bird in their hand and wishes to hold the bird securely enough so that it cannot fly away and yet gently enough so that it will not be harmed. Putting this analogy into practice will assist the fencer in relaxing the foil hand, and preventing the development of unnecessary muscle fatigue.

Preparatory Position

The preparatory position, sometimes referred to as the position of attention, appears to be a very formal pose for fencers. Fencers should assume this stance while waiting for the command "on guard." It is generally assumed during competition at any time play is stopped for any reason. This position

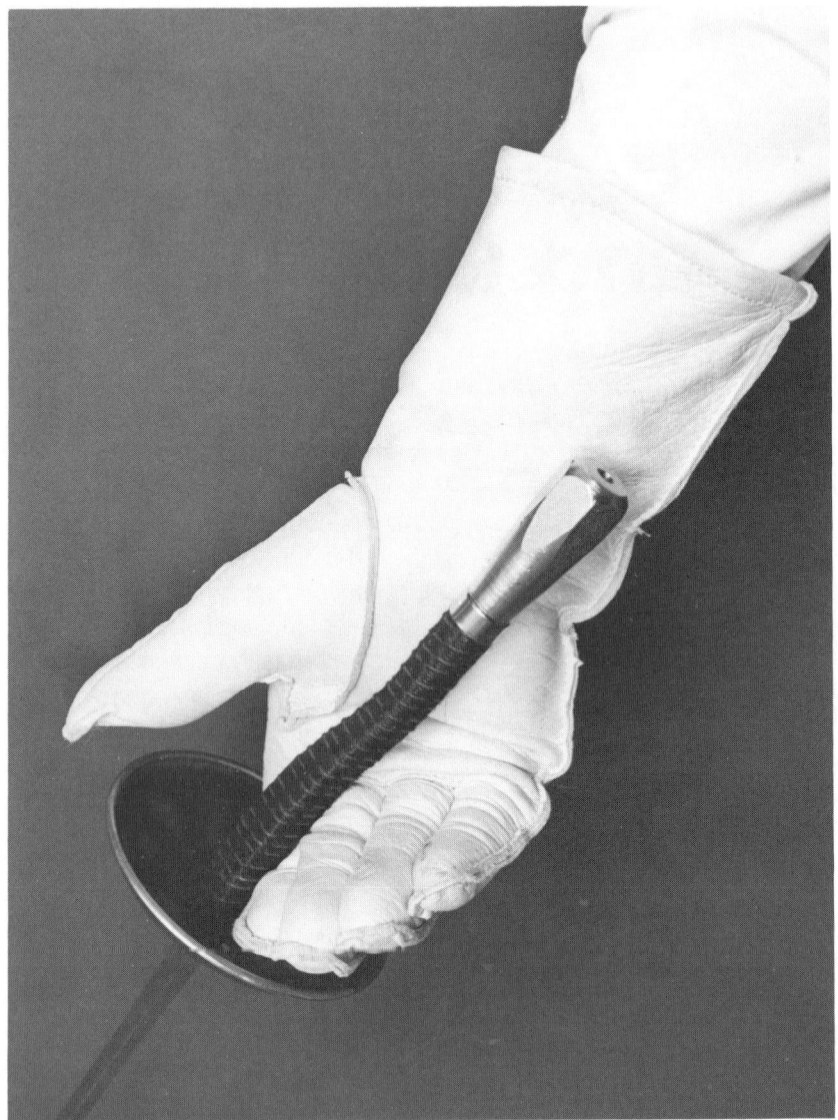

3.1 Grip Across Hand

is easily attained by standing erect and rotating the forward foot laterally 90 degrees. The forearm and foil are extended over the forward foot at approximately a 45 degree angle to the torso. The non-foil arm is placed in a position of easy extension behind the body at the same approximate angle as the foil arm. The fencer's head rotates to look over the foil arm

III. BASIC SKILLS AND MOBILITY 13

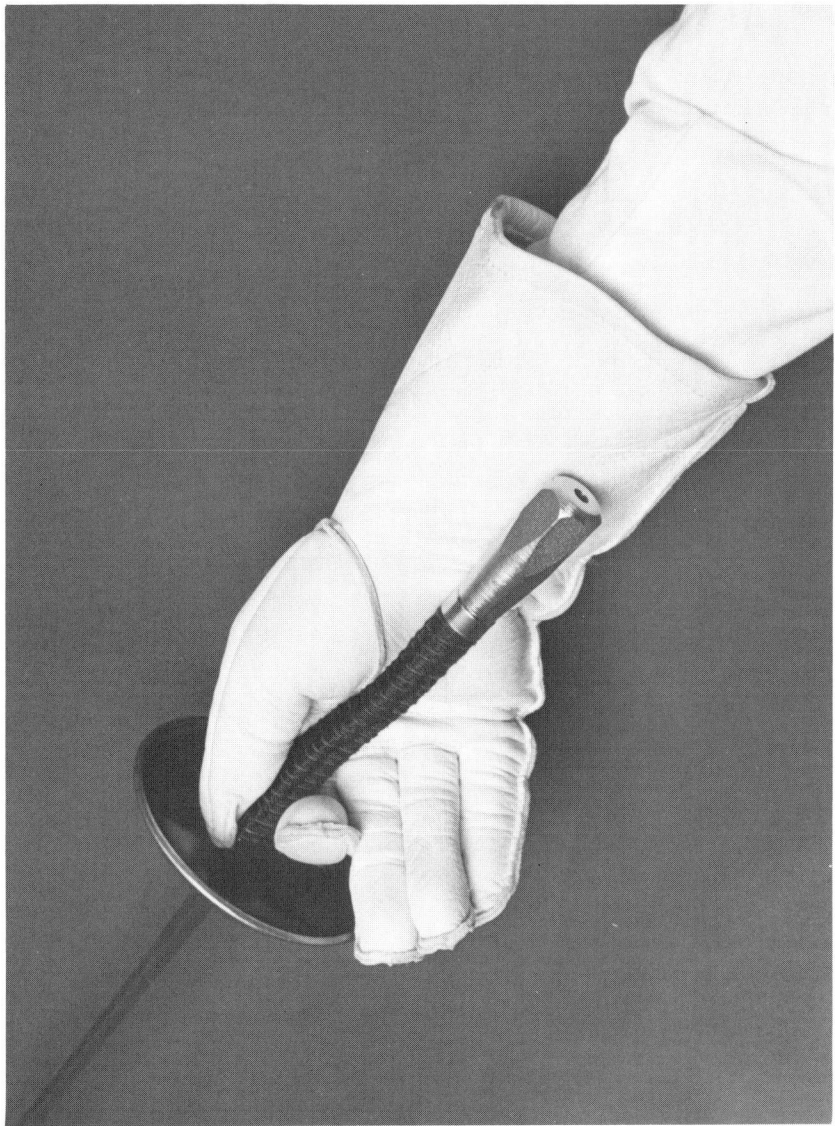

3.2 Thumb and index Finger

directly at the opponent (*Fig. 3.4*). This position of readiness allows the fencer to engage in the first eye contact and to begin to size up the opponent psychologically.

The sport of modern fencing has many examples of courtesy, some of which have evolved historically from the dueling era. One such display of

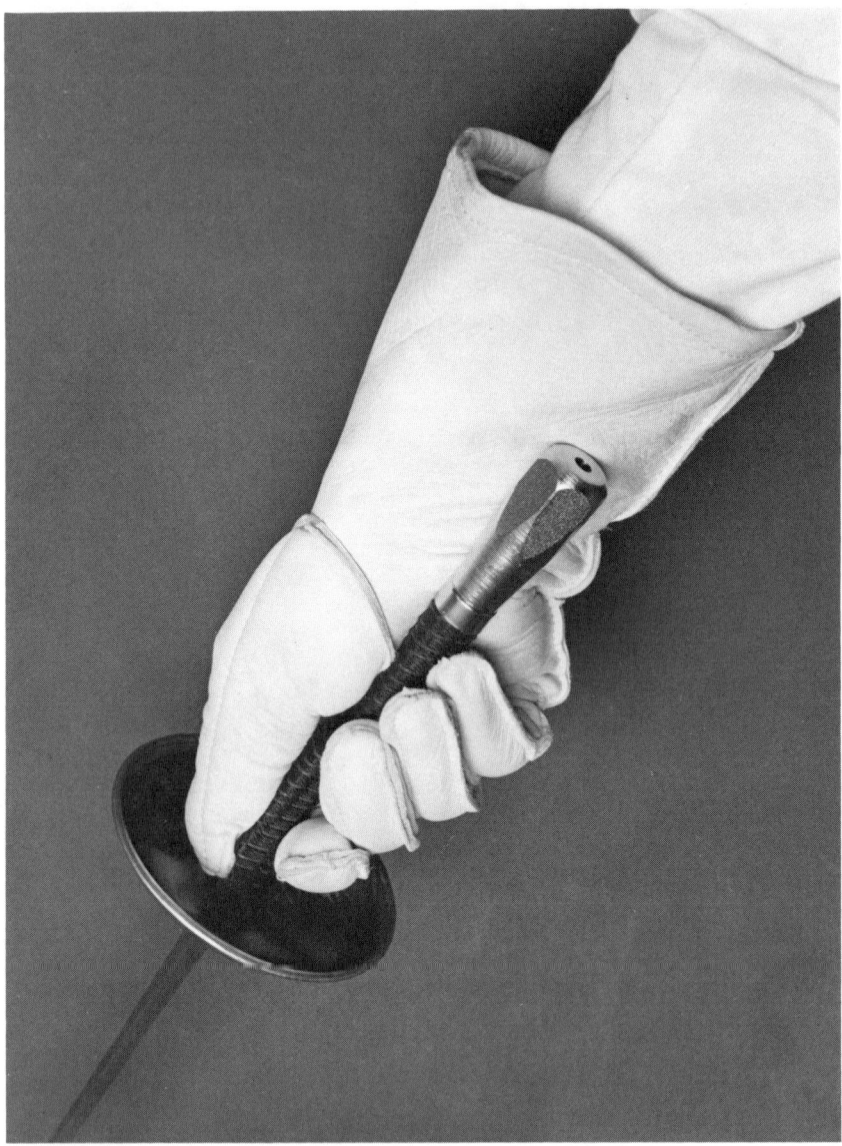

3.3 Entire Grip

courtesy in modern fencing is called the salute. Legend has it that during the era of dueling many of the duelists' swords had a crucifix etched on the hilt. Prior to the duel, opponents would kiss the crucifix and pray for divine guidance and victory. If they were dueling over the honor of a fair maiden, they would often tie her scarf or ribbon to the hilt and kiss them prior to the

II. BASIC SKILLS AND MOBILITY 15

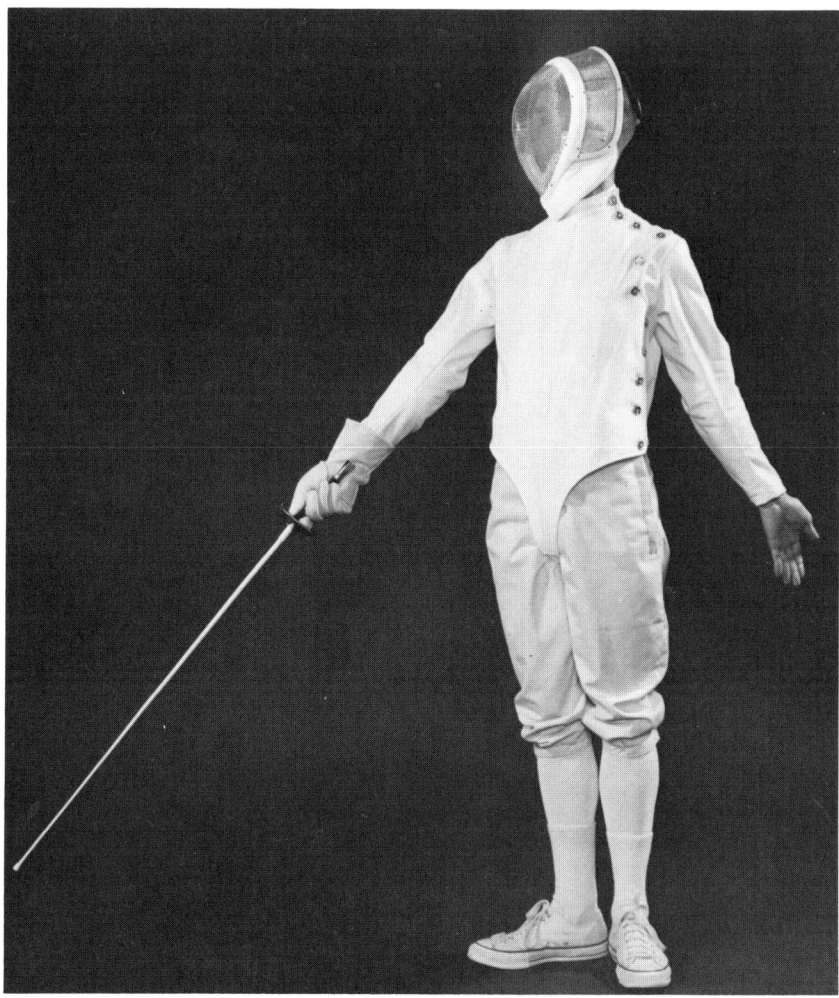

3.4 Attention

duel. This historical aspect of dueling has found its way into modern fencing and the salute is considered a necessary courteous acknowledgment of one's opponent. Some fencers will also salute the officials and the audience prior to competition; however, this is not a necessary application of the salute.

The salute is executed while the fencer is in the preparatory position (*Fig. 3.5*). The bell guard is brought to a position even with the fencer's mouth (*Fig. 3.6*). The arm is quickly returned to the starting position (*Fig. 3.7*).

16   THE FENCING BOOK

3.5 Phase 1—Salute

One only has to attend a fencing competition to become aware of the many variations to the salute. The choice of the salute is not important. What is important is poise and composure in executing the salute and the demonstration of courtesy to one's opponent.

III. BASIC SKILLS AND MOBILITY 17

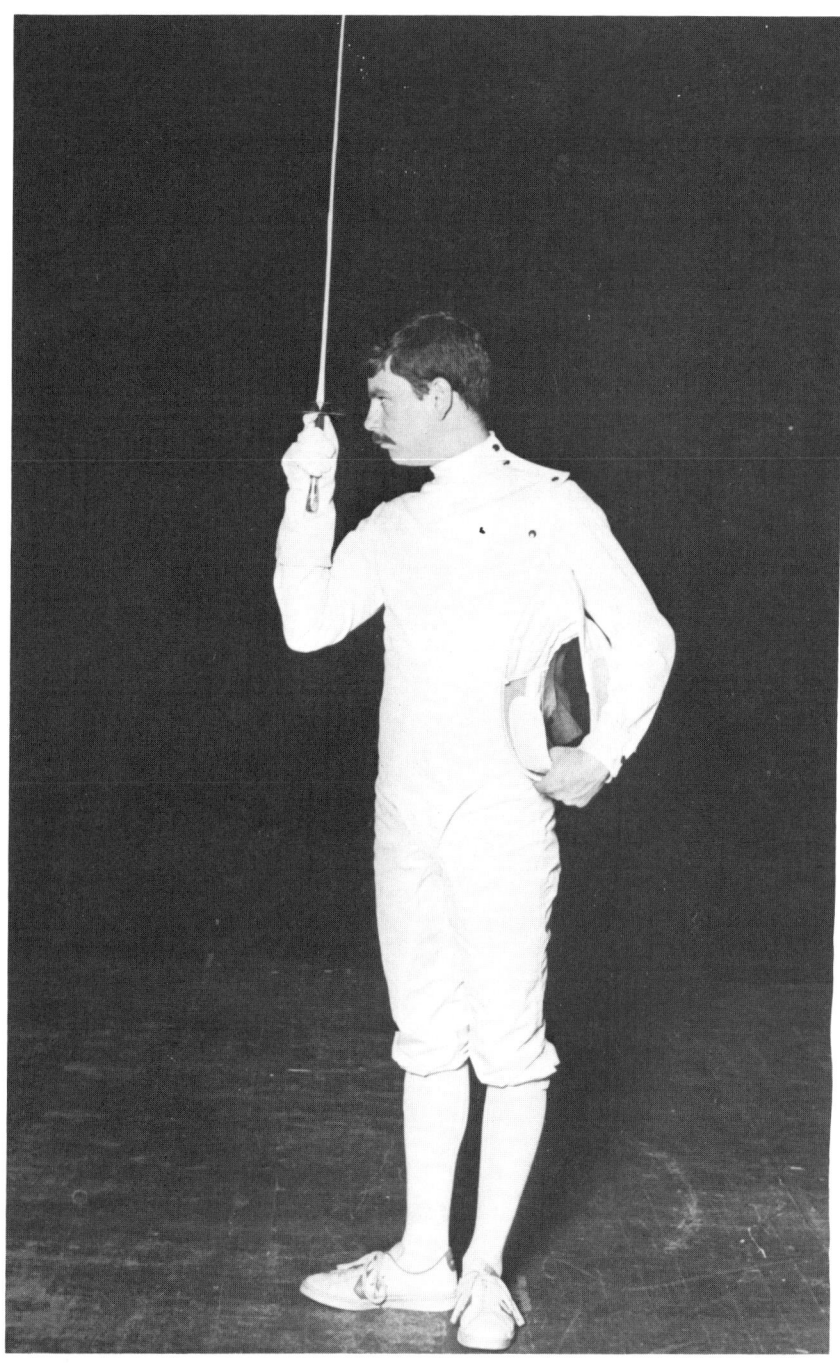

3.6 Phase 2—Salute

3.7 Phase 3—Salute

The Position of Guard

The position of guard is basic to all mobility in fencing (*Fig. 3.8*). One moves into the guard position from the preparatory position. It is in this position that the fencer will spend most of their time. It is extremely important that this skill be executed correctly and that the fencer discover a position which is as comfortable as possible.

III. BASIC SKILLS AND MOBILITY

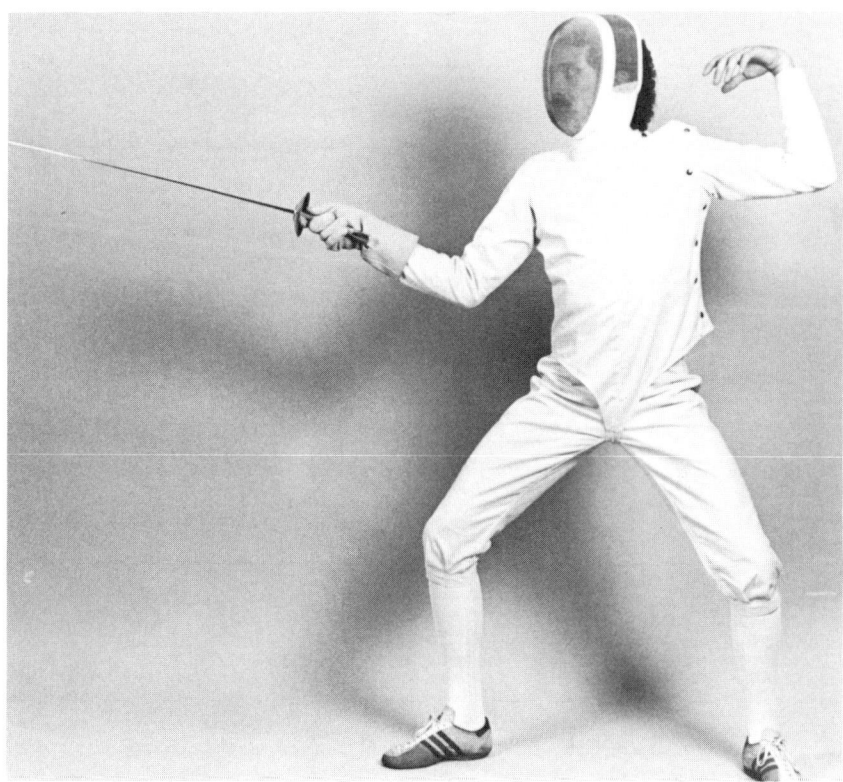

3.8 Guard Position

The forward foot is lifted and placed forward at a 90 degree angle approximately 18 to 24 inches from the rear foot (the distance will vary with the length of a fencer's legs). An important concept to remember when in the guard position is the wider one's base of support the more stability one has. However, if the base of support exceeds a fencer's shoulder width by more than 8-10 inches, it can also hinder mobility.

The weight of the body should be equally distributed on both feet in the guard position. This enables one to move forward or backward quickly without having to make a weight transfer prior to lifting the feet. The weight should be supported on the entire sole of each foot. The fencer should refrain from attempting to carry his/her weight on the ball of the foot only.

The position of the knees with regard to the feet is very important. The forward knee should be slightly behind the toes of that foot and centered over the instep of the foot. The rear leg should be positioned so that the knee is even with the toes but rotated slightly toward the inside of the foot. If

3.9 Front View of Guard

III. BASIC SKILLS AND MOBILITY

the rear knee is kept exactly over the instep of the foot, it has a tendency to pull the fencer's weight toward and onto the back foot, thus making it difficult for the fencer to retreat quickly. (In order to retreat, the fencer must make a weight transfer forward before being able to lift the rear foot.) The torso is kept in an erect position as the fencer's knees are flexed. The body should not be allowed to lean either forward toward the foil arm or backward away from one's opponent. The appearance should be that of a fencer sitting quite comfortably on an imaginary pedestal.

The foil arm is flexed so the forearm forms a 90 degree angle with the upper arm. The elbow is held six to eight inches or a hand's span away from the torso. The fencer holds the pommel of the foil snuggly against the inside of the wrist and the wrist is ulnar flexed so the point of the weapon is at the opponent's eye level. The foil hand should be held at chest height. Any attempt to hold it higher obstructs the fencer's view. The thumb of the foil hand should be turned to approximately a two o'clock position for right-handed fencers or a ten o'clock for left-handed fencers. This places the hand in a slightly supinated position for the guard. The elbow of the foil arm should be medially adducted so one can cover as much of the valid target area as possible with the foil arm (*Fig. 3.9*).

The position of the non-foil arm has a rather colorful past in the history of fencing. Legend tells us that when dueling was at its peak, the free hand or non-foil arm often carried a dagger or a buckler, which was used for blocking the attacking blades. In other contests the non-foil arm was carried to show one's opponent that the free hand was not harboring an additional weapon.

In the sixteenth century dueling was banned by many of the leading monarchs of Europe. Despite the ban, many a high-spirited young man continued to pursue dueling as a method of defending his honor. In order to evade the laws which prohibited dueling, they would duel in the dark. A lantern was held high by each duelist in the free hand so his opponent could see him, or at least see an outline of his torso. Thus they were able to duel.

In the sport today, since we neither use a dagger for blocking nor a lantern to outline our torso, the non-foil arm is carried in this position to assist the fencer in maintaining balance and controlling movement. When moving to the guard position, the action is started by shoulder abduction with the palm in a supinated position. The arm is elevated to a point where it is parallel to the floor; at that time the elbow is flexed, resulting in the forearm being perpendicular to the floor. Both the wrist and fingers of the non-foil arm are relaxed and the hand allowed to point casually toward the head. When moving from the preparatory position to the position of guard or

3.10 Advance

vice versa, the above sequence of action should be done simultaneously and as smoothly and effortlessly as possible.

Mobility

There are many forms of mobility which one can explore in the sport of fencing. The poise and control with which one performs these movements will determine in part the success one has in fencing. All systematic forward and backward movement is initiated from the guard position.

The Advance

A systematic stepping movement toward one's opponent is called an advance (*Fig. 3.10*). The advance is initiated by lifting the forward foot and placing it ten to twelve inches forward, insuring that the feet are still perpendicular to each other. After the forward foot touches the floor, the rear foot is lifted and drawn forward close to the original guard stance. One must take care not to allow the base of support to become too narrow. These movements are repeated until the desired distance is gained.

3.11 Retreat

The Retreat

The backward movement or movement away from one's opponent is called the retreat (*Fig. 3.11*). It is initiated by lifting the rear foot and placing it ten to twelve inches to the rear, insuring that the feet are still perpendicular to each other. After the rear foot touches the floor, the forward foot is lifted and closed to the guard stance. These movements are repeated until the desired distance has been established. Care should be taken not to allow one's base of support to become too narrow.

As one advances and/or retreats, the shoulder and hips remain on the same horizontal plane. There is no vertical movement of the torso with each step. The tempo of advance and retreat should be constantly varied in order to disguise one's plans for gaining ground and/or attacking.

3.12 Lunge (Stationary)

The Lunge

Another form of mobility is called the lunge (*Fig. 3.12*). It is also referred to by some masters as the development. The lunge is the quickest way to close the distance to one's opponent. One must think of the lunge as beginning with the tip of one's foil. It is as though someone has grasped the tip of the foil and is pulling it rapidly forward, causing a rapid extension of the foil arm with the body following (*Fig. 3.13*). The lunge should always have the extension of the foil arm (a thrust) as its primary movement (*Fig. 3.14*). Following the rapid extension of this foil arm toward the opponent's target, the forward foot is lifted and kicked toward the opponent simultaneously as the rear leg extends. As the leg movements are executed, the non-foil arm is flung backward away from the torso to a position nearly parallel to the extended rear leg. This action, coupled with the right foot touching the floor, concludes the lunge. Flinging of the rear arm back to a position of easy extension aids the fencer in two ways. It exemplifies Newton's Third Law—for every acting force there should be an equal and opposite reacting force. The action plays an important part in the maintenance of body balance in

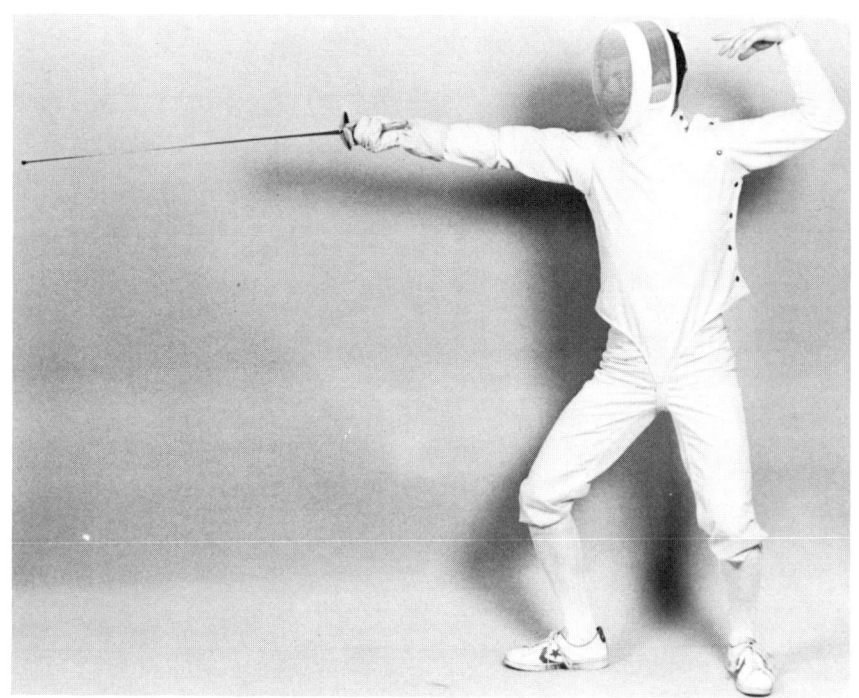

3.13 Thrust

3.14 Lunge (Strobe)

3.15 Thrust Lunge Recovery Fwd.—Lunge

the execution of the lunge. Secondly, the rapid flexion during the recovery to the guard position assists in moving the body mass back to the base of support used in the guard position.

Once in the lunge position, the weight should be equally distributed on both feet. As the fencer moves to the lunge, the knee of the forward foot should be directly over the instep of the forward foot. If the knee is allowed to move to a position in front of the instep, there is a tendency for the fencer to have more weight on the forward foot than the back. This will slow down the fencer's ability to recover to the guard. If the knee is kept behind the instep, it is a good indication the fencer has overstepped his/her lunge and will have a difficult time recovering.

III. BASIC SKILLS AND MOBILITY   27

The Recovery

The recovery from the lunge to the guard position can be made either backward or forward. If one wishes to resume the original position prior to the lunge attack, the fencer should recover backward to the guard position. The fencer pushes off with the forward foot while rapidly flexing the non-foil arm. This rapid flexion of the foil arm and push off with the forward foot allows the fencer to move their body mass backward and settle back into the original guard position.

If one's opponent has retreated as a defense to the lunge attack, the fencer should recover forward (*Fig. 3.15*). By recovering forward and maintaining the extended foil arm, one can continue the attack by lunging again. To recover forward, the non-foil arm is quickly flexed at the elbow and adducted at the shoulder, while the rear leg is flexed and pulled forward to the original guard stance. Every effort should be made to keep the foil arm extended. The fencer is now ready to advance, execute an additional lunge or any other appropriate blade action.

The Advance-Lunge

The advance-lunge (*Fig. 3.16*) is another technique that can be effectively used against an opponent who retreats against each attack. The advance-lunge is a combination of a very quick advance step followed by an immediate lunge. In the advance-lunge, the foil arm must be extended at the very beginning of the advance step. This is the actual beginning of the attack, and the extended arm threatening the opponent gives the attack the right of way. It must remain extended throughout the advance-lunge. Any withdrawal of that arm leaves the fencer in a position to receive a hit. In executing the advance-lunge, the arm is extended and the advance step is taken. As soon as the rear leg closes for the guard position, the fencer immediately springs forward into a lunge. This attack is an excellent one to use against an opponent who continually retreats with each attack or with one who maintains a fencing distance beyond that which could be closed with a thrust-lunge attack.

Ballestra

The ballestra or jump lunge is another type of mobility. When combined with an extended blade action, it forms a beautiful attack (*Fig. 3.17*). In executing the ballestra, the fencer first extends the foil arm. The forward foot is lifted while rapidly pushing off with the rear foot to execute a jump forward. The primary purpose of this jump is to gain distance, not height. Both feet land

3.16 Advance Lunge

3.17 Ballestra

3.18 Fleché

on the floor simultaneously. Immediately utilizing the momentum gained from the jump, the fencer springs forward into a lunge attack. The element of surprise, coupled with a forceful momentum toward the opponent, makes the ballestra a most effective attack.

The Fleché

The fleché or arrow is a running attack and is usually considered an advanced skill (*Fig. 3.18*). As in any movement of fencing, the element of surprise is extremely important to the success of a specific movement; therefore, it is unwise to attempt to use the fleché frequently. The fleché is executed by extending the foil arm toward the opponent and leaning so the knee of the forward foot is well beyond the toes of that foot. At the extreme position of the lean, there will appear to be almost a straight line between the point of the foil and the foot of the rear leg. As one leans forward and body weight starts to move forward, the left foot swings past the right foot and the fencer continues running at the opponent in an effort to score. It is imperative that the attacker run by the opponent. The opponent should not be touched with anything but the foil. Many have referred to this attack as a 'do or die' attack because should it miss or be parried, the attacker is in a very vulnerable position as he/she runs by the opponent. It is best to keep the running attack as short as possible, perhaps no further away from the fencer than that distance which could be easily covered by a ballestra or an advance lunge. Attempting a running attack from a distance greater than these two gives the opponent an excellent opportunity to set a defense for the attack.

Evaluation Questions

1. What are the purposes of the thumb and index finger when gripping the foil?
2. How did the salute originate?
3. What is the most important factor in determining the effectiveness of mobility?
4. What is the fleché?
5. Is there vertical movement of the torso during the advance and the retreat?
6. What is the purpose of the movement of the non-foil arm during the lunge and recovery?

CHAPTER FOUR

Blade Actions

The actions of the blade in the sport of fencing are essentially what the sport is all about. The forms of mobility discussed previously mean very little if one does not have the proper control, finesse, speed, and determination when using the foil. The actions of the blade can be described as either offensive in nature or defensive in nature. These offensive and defensive lines are normally divided into four general areas: high inside (fourth position), high outside (sixth position), low inside (seventh position), and low outside (eighth position). When one assumes the position of guard and holds the foil in what is often referred to as the central position, the four lines of attack are easily distinguishable (*Fig. 4.1*). (Positions one, two, three and five are not discussed because they are used in sabre and épée fencing—not foil, to which this book is directed.)

These offensive and defensive lines are not stationary. They move with the position of the fencer's foil arm and hand. All attacks made on the palm side of the foil arm are called attacks to the inside line, while all to the back side of the hand are attacks to the outside line. The high line and the low line are divided also at the hand position. Any attack made above the hand is referred to as a high line attack, and any attack made below the hand a low line attack. The fencer may elect to close a specific line or open a specific line depending on the strategy one plans to employ. For example, if a fencer adducts the foil arm horizontally approximately four to six inches while in the guard position, the inside line closes (*Fig. 4.2*). If the foil arm is abducted horizontally approximately four to six inches while in the guard position, it closes the outside line (*Fig. 4.3*). One can ascertain by closing these lines that they have completely opened the opposing line. Upon elevation of the foil arm, the high line is closed (*Fig. 4.4*), or upon depression of the foil arm, the low line can be closed (*Fig. 4.5*). In examining the hand positions for the lines of attack, we refer to two positions of the hand known as pronation and supination. Pronation implies rotation of the hand so the palm is down toward the floor. Supination implies rotation of the hand so the palm is up toward the ceiling.

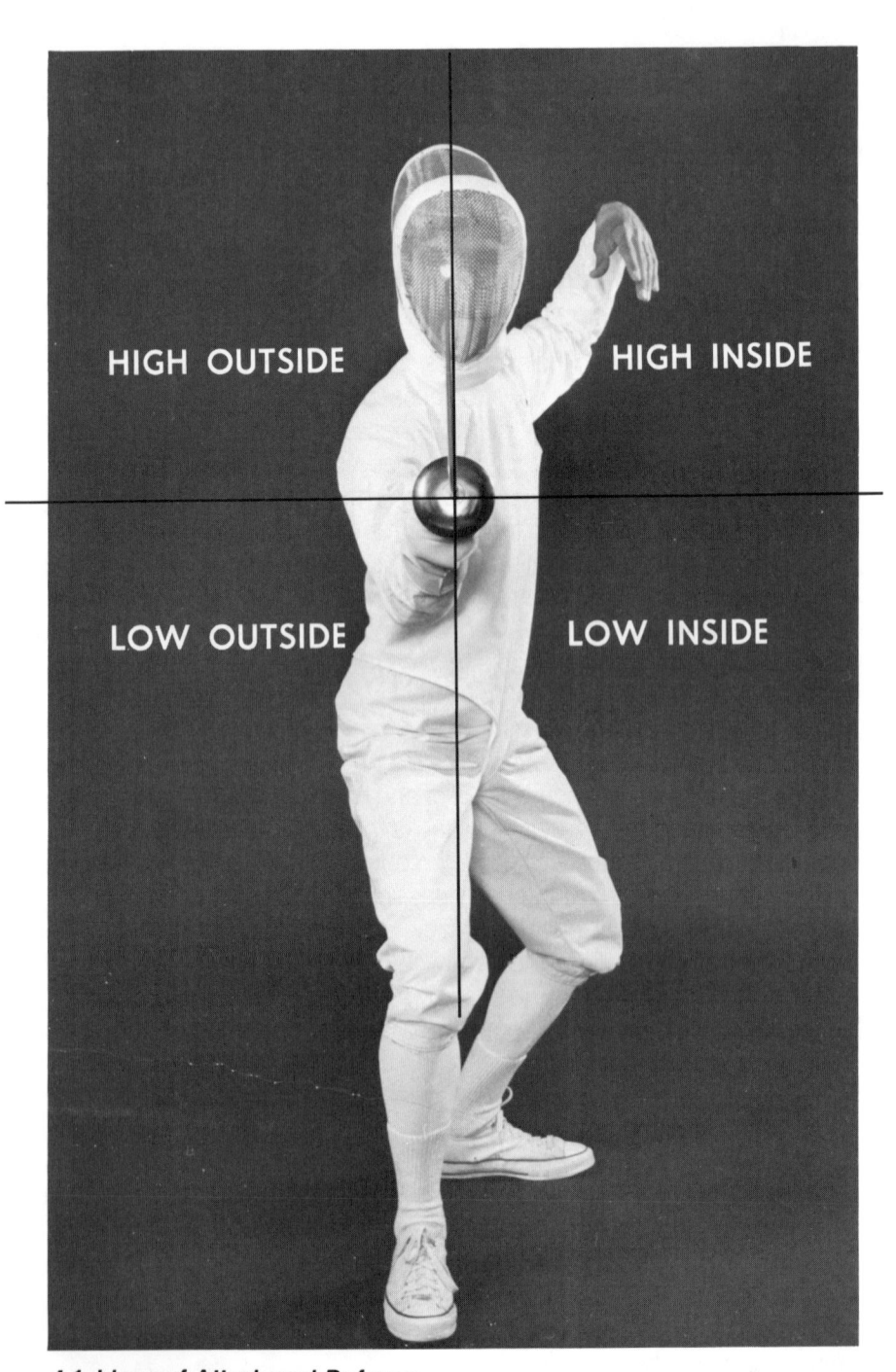

4.1 Lines of Attack and Defense

IV. BLADE ACTIONS

4.2 Close Inside Line

4.3 Close Outside Line

IV. BLADE ACTIONS

4.4 Close High Line

4.5 Close Low Line

IV. BLADE ACTIONS

4.6 Engagement

The position of the hand for fourth line should be the same as the position of the hand for the central guard position. The thumb is at twelve o'clock for both right- and left-handed fencers. In both fourth and sixth positions, the point of the foil should be above the bell guard. The hand position for sixth line is with the palm supinated slightly. If one is a right-handed fencer, the thumb should be approximately at three o'clock. If one is a left-handed fencer, the thumb should be rotated to a position at nine o'clock. In seventh position the hand is supinated with the thumb at three o'clock for right-handed fencers and nine o'clock for left-handed fencers. To put the hand in eighth position correctly, one supinates the hand slightly with the thumb at two o'clock for right-handed fencers and ten o'clock for left-handed fencers. In both seventh and eighth positions, the point of the foil should be below the bell guard.

Any time the foils of two opposing fencers are in contact, it is called an engagement (*Fig. 4.6*). The fencers are in a position of guard and of readiness for combat.

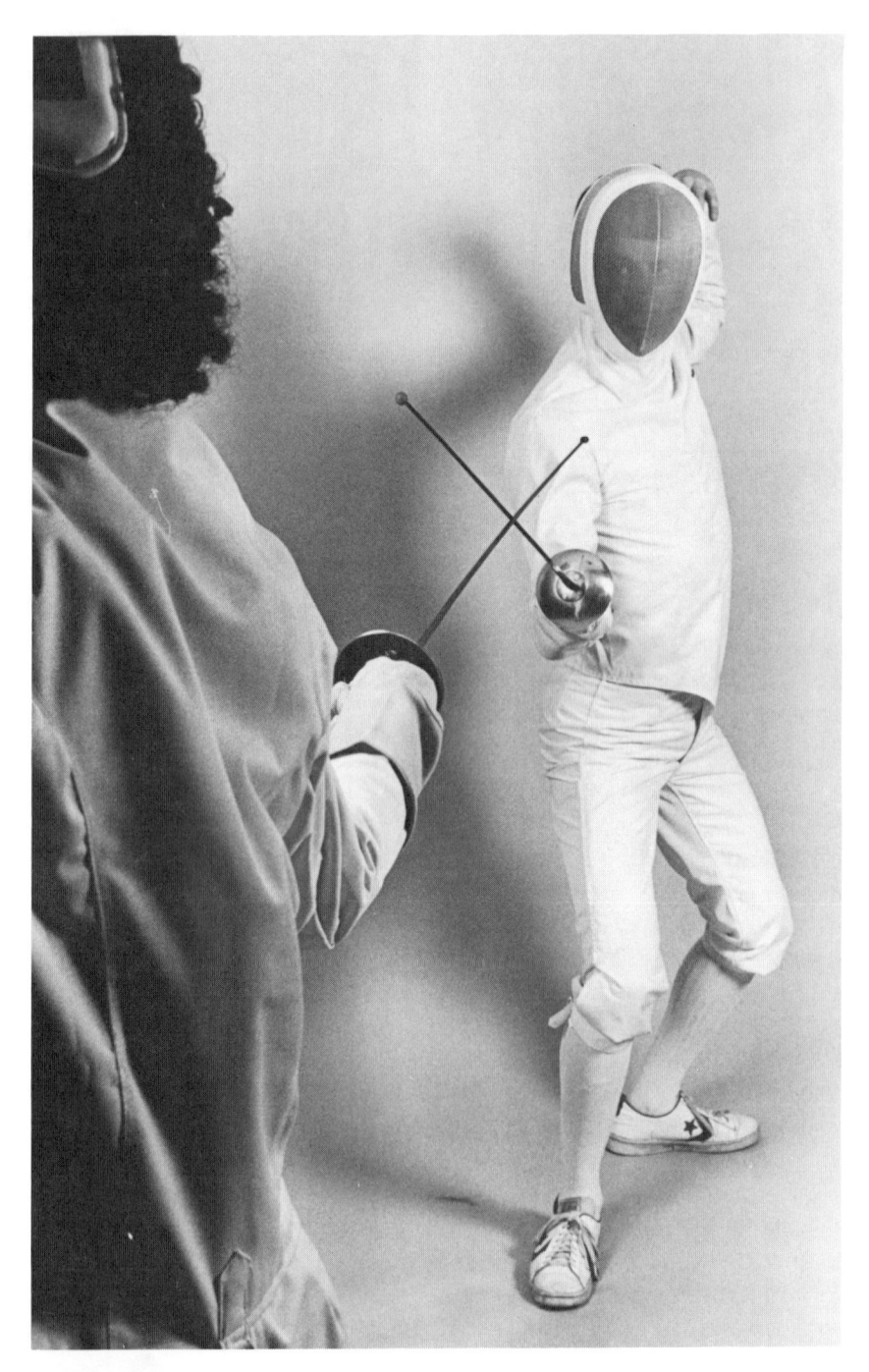

4.7 Engagement in High Inside

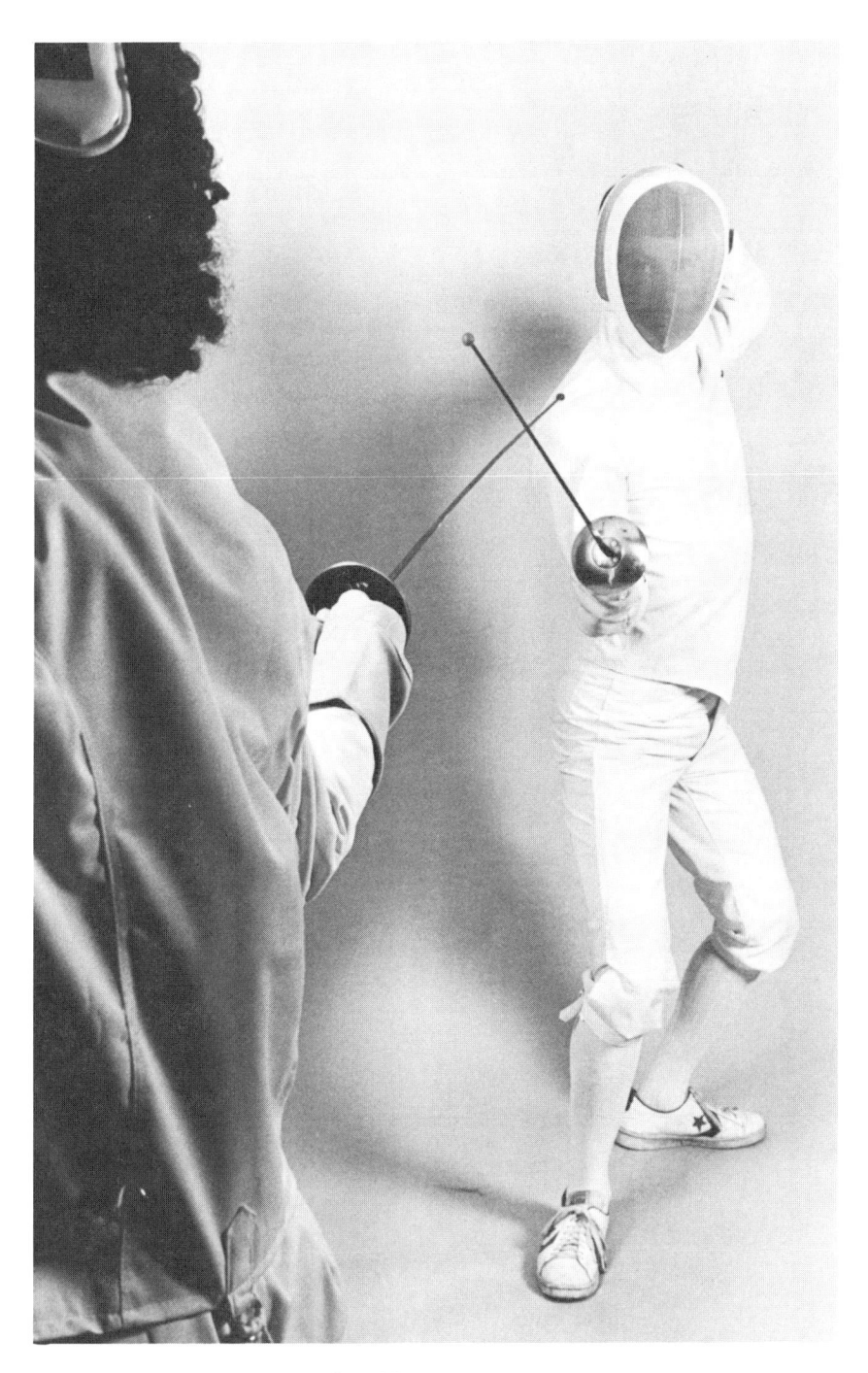

IV. BLADE ACTIONS 39

4.8 Engagement in High Outside

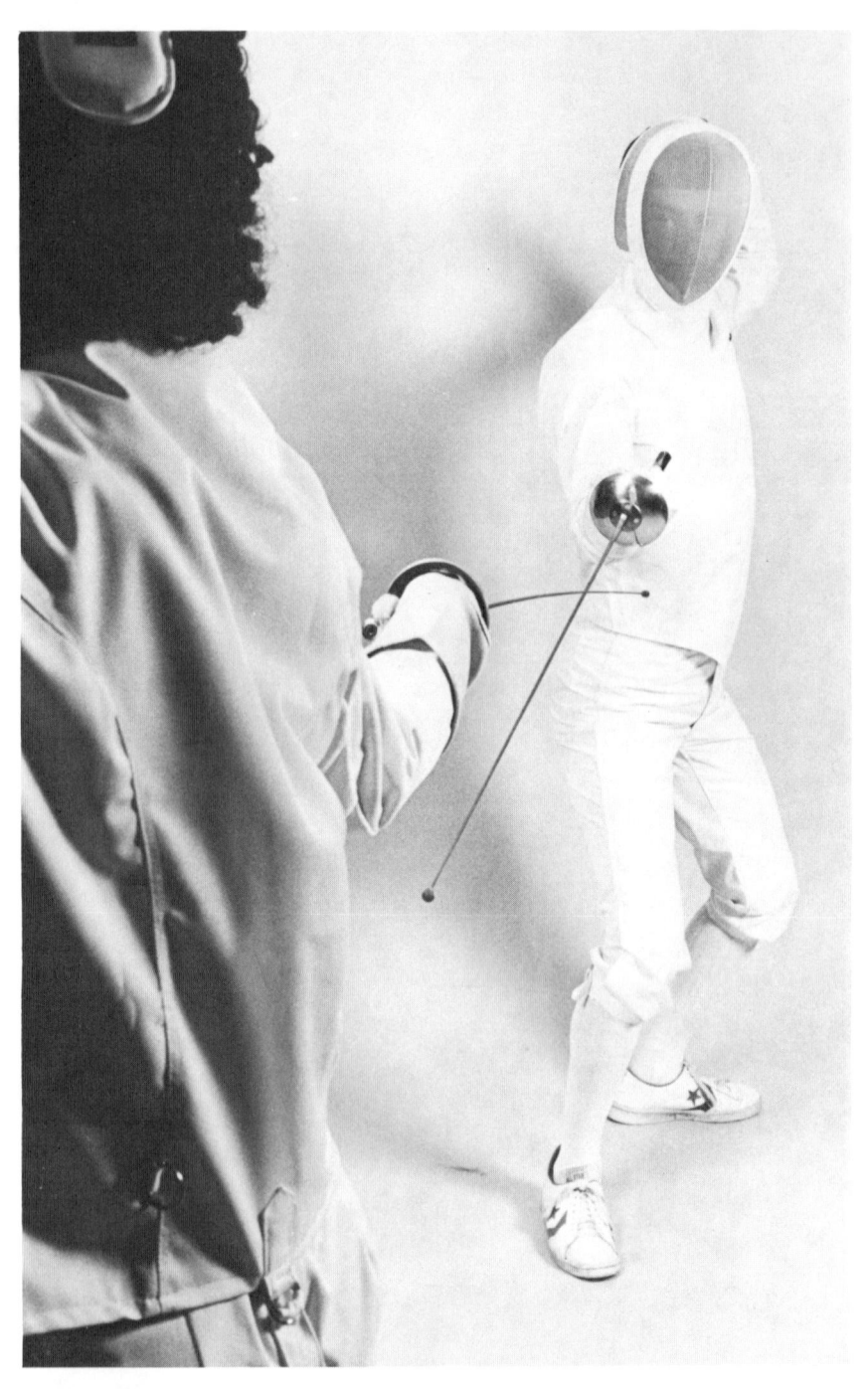

4.9 Engagement in Low Inside

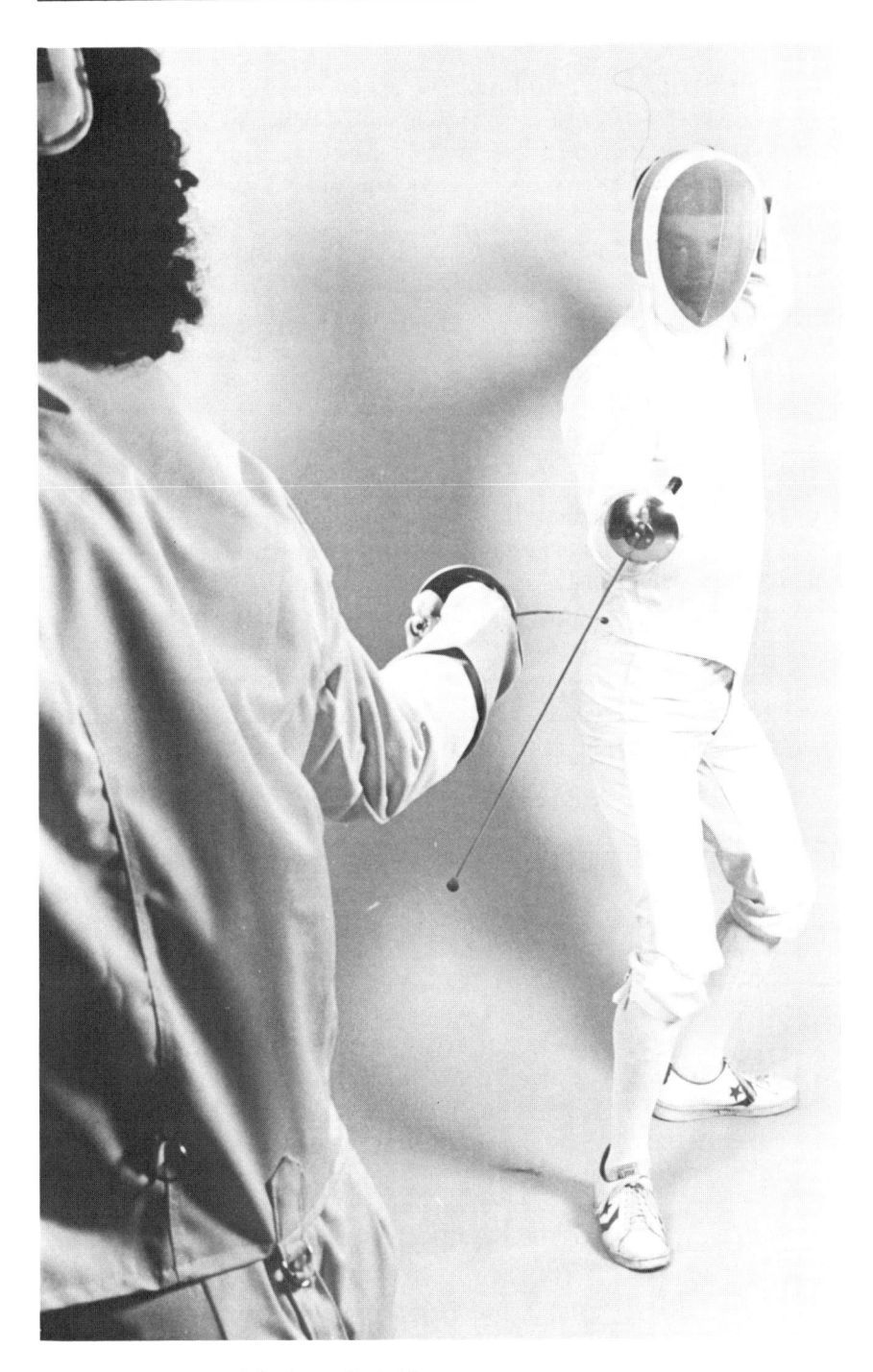

IV. BLADE ACTIONS 41

4.10 Engagement in Low Outside

When two fencers are on guard and their foils are crossed on the palm side of the hand with the points up, they are engaged in the high inside line (*Fig. 4.7*). When two fencers are on guard and their blades are touching and crossing on the back side of the hand, they are engaged in the high outside line (*Fig. 4.9*). When the blades of two fencers are crossed on the back side of the hand and the points are down, the fencers are said to be engaged in a low outside line (*Fig. 4.10*). When a right- and left-handed fencer engage, the reference to their engagement is relative to whether they are on offense or defense.

An engagement is not mandatory; in fact, a great number of fencers prefer to fence in absence of the blade. This implies there is no contact with the opposing blade.

The Target

The valid target for scoring touches in both men's and women's foil excludes the limbs and the head. It is limited to the trunk of the body reaching from the top of the upper edge of the collar down the entire front of the fencer including the groin. It extends on the sides from shoulder seam to shoulder seam of each sleeve on the front and the back, and from the lower portion of the sleeve seam to the waist on the sides. In essence, the entire jacket excluding the sleeves is a valid target (*Fig. 4.11*). The bib of the mask is not considered a valid target.

OFFENSIVE BLADE ACTIONS

An offensive blade action or an attack is defined as the "initial offensive action executed by extending the arm and continuously threatening the opponent's valid target" (USFA Rules Book,) (*Fig. 4.12*). The number of blade actions or combinations of blade actions one can use to comprise an attack is unlimited. The fencer who initiates offensive action is said to have the right of way. The fencer's opponent must first stop the attack with a parry or retreat from the attack before making an attack. It is wise to remember that the blade action between two fencers is often referred to as a conversation of blades. One fencer extends the foil, threatens the opponent's target, has right of way, and attacks. With this movement the fencer says, "I am going to hit you." The opponent stops the attack with the blade by using a parry, or by retreating from the attack. This action says, "No, you're not." If the opponent immediately counterattacks or ripostes, he/she is in essence saying, "I'm going to hit you." Therefore, there is a continual exchange of attacks and defenses with one person attacking and

IV. BLADE ACTIONS 43

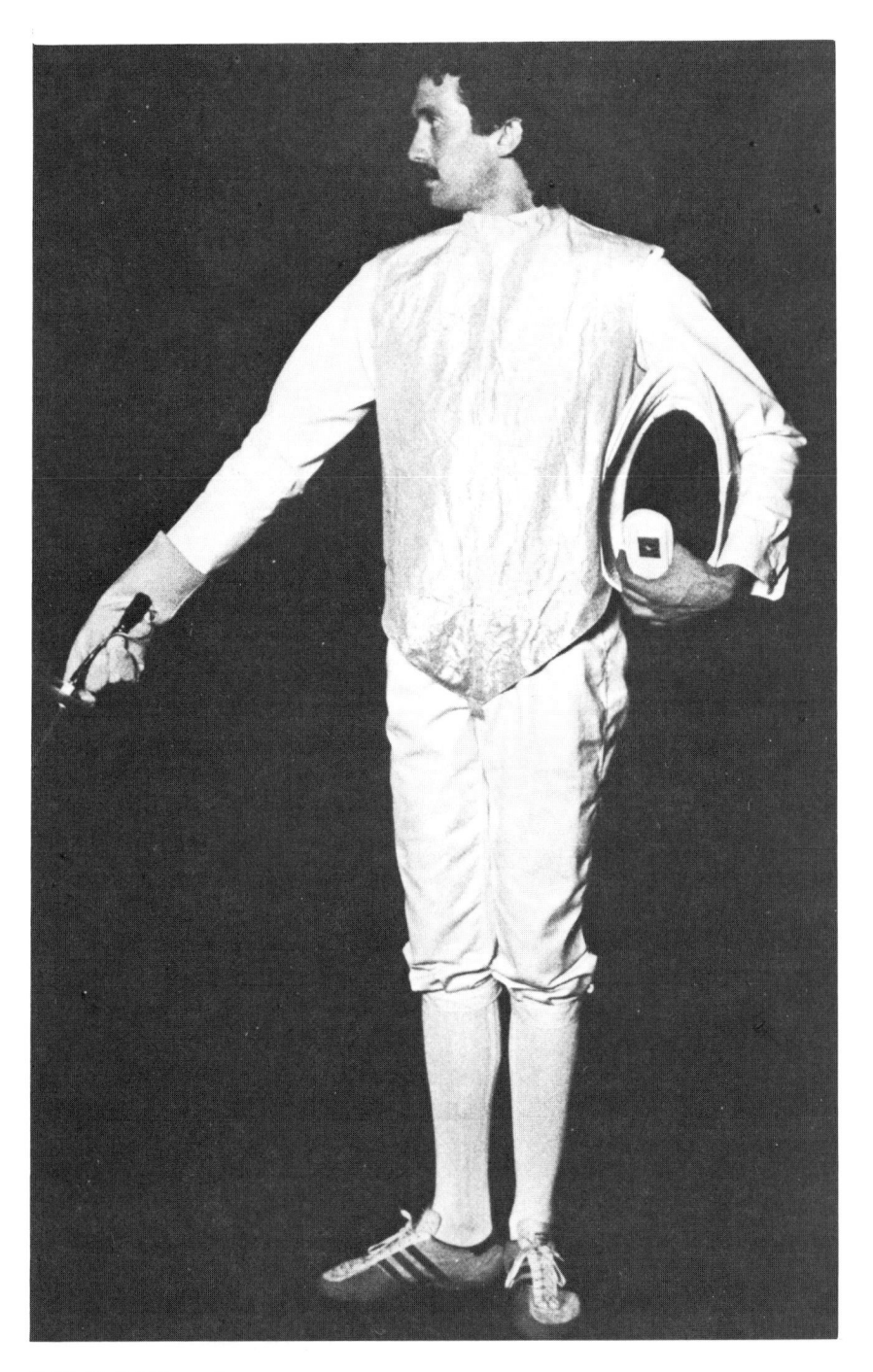

***4.11* Valid Target**

4.12 Thrust—Threatening Valid Target

4.13 Simple Attack Thrust Lunge

IV. BLADE ACTIONS 45

the other defending and counterattacking. In learning social amenities we are often taught that it is improper for two people to speak at once. This courtesy can also be applied to the sport of fencing. One should avoid attacking at the same time as one's opponent. One should also avoid initiating an attack just because one's opponent started an attack.

Simple Attacks

A simple attack consists of a single blade movement. The execution of this movement is done very rapidly and the attack is made into a line that is open. The three types of simple attacks are:
- The thrust, or direct attack, which is a rapid extension of the foil arm in the line of engagement. This simplest of all attacks involves a quick extension of the foil arm. At the completion of the extension, the tip of the foil should be slightly below the bell guard. The extension may be followed by a lunge if the distance to one's opponent requires it (*Fig. 4.13*).
- The disengage, or cut-under, which moves the fencer's blade from a closed line to an open line by passing the tip of the foil under the opponent's blade (*Fig. 4.14a-d*). Execution of the disengage starts with an extension of the foil arm. The attacking fencer should remember to keep the foil tip as close as possible to the opponent's bell guard during the disengage. This blade movement should be done with rotary action at the wrist, not elevation and depression of the forearm. The tip of the blade forms a small semicircle or "V" during this action.
- The coupé, or cut-over, moves the fencer's blade from a closed line to an open line by passing the foil over the opponent's weapon (*Fig. 4.15a-c*). It is important to remember that this particular attack will be more effective when used against an opponent who carries their blade in a rather low position. Rotary action of the wrist should be used in the coupé. Elevation and depression of the forearm leave the fencer in a vulnerable position.

Multiples of the coupé and disengage may be used in an attempt to confuse one's opponent. These will be discussed more extensively in the area of compound attacks.

Compound Attacks

A compound attack consists of two or more blade movements. The first blade movement or movements are used as a prelude to the actual attack and have the specific purpose of drawing the opponent out of line or into a defensive movement, thus opening a line for an attack. When executing a compound attack, it is important for the fencer to have the right of way. To do so one must extend that foil arm as the first movement of the compound

4.14a *The Disengage Attack*

4.14b *The Disengage Attack*

IV. BLADE ACTIONS 47

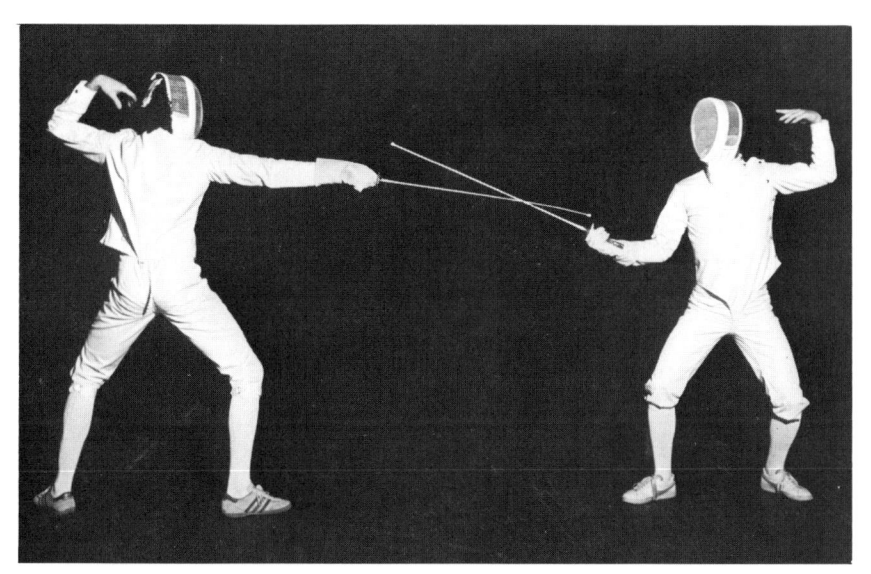

4.14c The Disengage Attack

4.14d The Disengage Attack

48　THE FENCING BOOK

4.15a The Coupé Attack

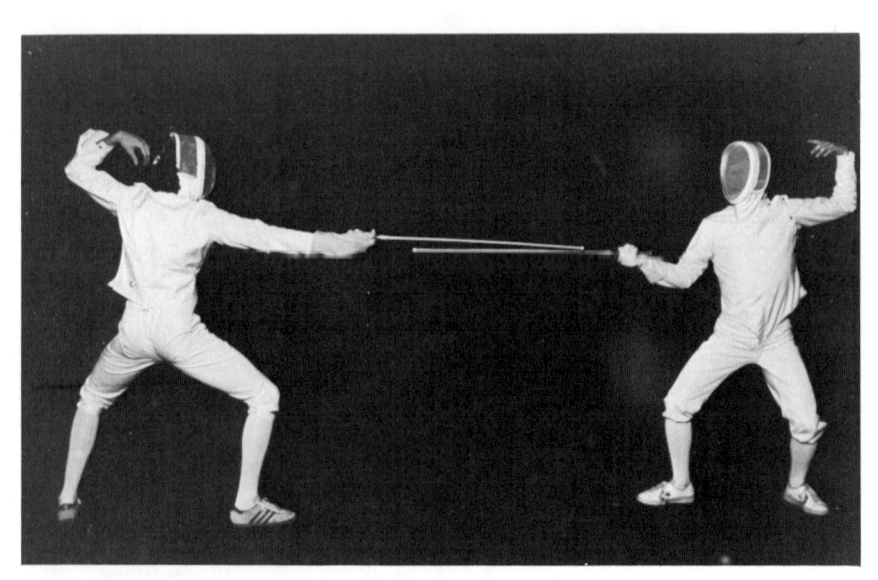

4.15b The Coupé Attack

IV. BLADE ACTIONS 49

4.15c The Coupé Attack

attack is executed. Any effort to flex the foil arm or withdraw it during the attack causes the fencer to forfeit the right of way.

Examples of introductory movements are the beat, press, and feint, any one of which the attacker may use in order to evoke a response from the opponent.

The Beat Attack

The beat attack is a sharp rap with the midsection of one's blade on the foible or midsection of the opponent's blade. This sharp rap must be followed immediately by a thrust and lunge. The sharp rap, in addition to opening the line for attack, will delay the opponent's ability to defend. Often the beat will cause the opponent to come back quickly to defend the line and the opposite line will suddenly be opened. In that case, the attacker should disengage and attack to the open line. Maintaining the element of surprise in this attack is crucial.

The Press Attack

The press attack is an application of continual pressure against the opponent's blade, using the midsection of the attacking blade against the foible or the midsection of the defending blade. This can be followed immediately with a thrust and lunge. This pressure, in addition to opening a line for an attack, will at times cause the opponent to overreact with a defensive movement, in opposition to the press. When one experiences the returning pressure from the opponent, one should disengage to the opposite line. This press attack can be very nicely combined with both the disengage and the coupé to an open line.

The Feint

The feint or false attack is made with the specific purpose of evoking a response, usually a parry, from the opponent. The attempt to parry a feint will result in further opening the line opposite the one in which the feint was made. The attacker deceives the defending blade with either a coupé or a disengage and continues into an open line.

Two beautiful attacks combining the feint and disengage are the one-two and the one-two-three. These attacks, when executed with finesse and skill, comprise two of the more effective attacks in the sport of fencing.

The one-two attack involves an extension of the foil arm in a line for the sole purpose of evoking a defensive parry response from one's opponent (*Fig. 4.16*). As one's opponent moves to catch the blade on that extension, a rapid disengage is done followed by a lunge into another line. Two key concepts, when executing the one-two attack, are:
- As one disengages, the foil arm must be maintained in an extended position;
- As one executes the disengage, the foil point should be kept in as close to the opponent's bell guard as possible, so as to threaten the target continually.

The one-two-three attack is an extension of the one-two in that the attack begins with an extension in an open line (*Fig. 4.17*). As the opponent moves to defend and parry the attacking blade, a quick disengage is done into the opposite open line. As the opponent moves back in an attempt to parry the second feint, a disengage back to the original line is completed with a rapid lunge following. The attacker has executed a feint, double disengage and lunge. The foil arm must be maintained in an extended position during the feint and the disengages. The disengages must be done with the point as close to the opponent's bell guard as possible. One of the most important factors in the success of these two attacks is the opponent's reactions to feints. If the opponent does not react to feints, then one should opt for other attacks, such as a straight or simple attack with lightning speed.

These are not all the compound attacks. Many combinations of blade actions can be created to form effective attacks. It is important for a fencer to become creative and to apply the basic skills in varying combinations to

IV. BLADE ACTIONS

see what works best. One's strategy is limited only by lack of imagination and creativity.

A fencer also should take time to study their opponent in action in order to detect habitual movement patterns or blade actions. The fencer should then devise techniques to take advantage of these patterns when confronted with them during a bout.

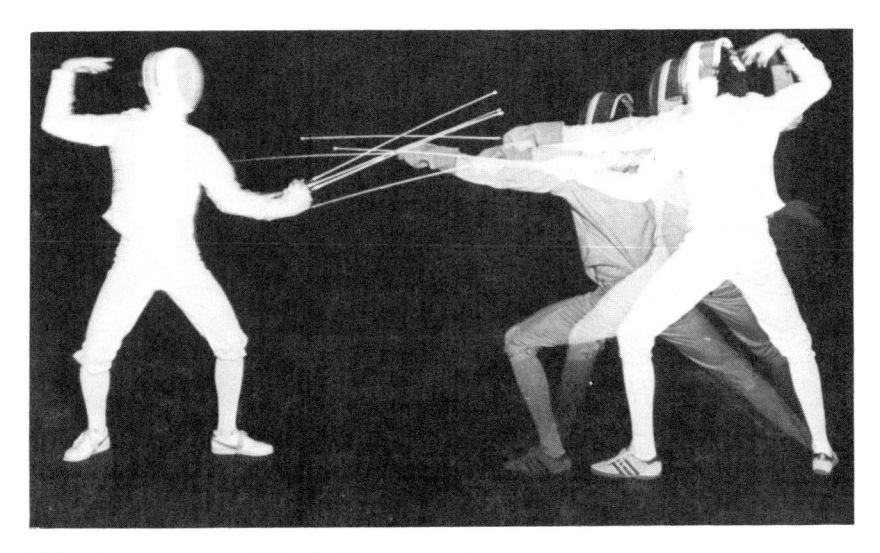

4.16 The One-Two Attack (Disengage)

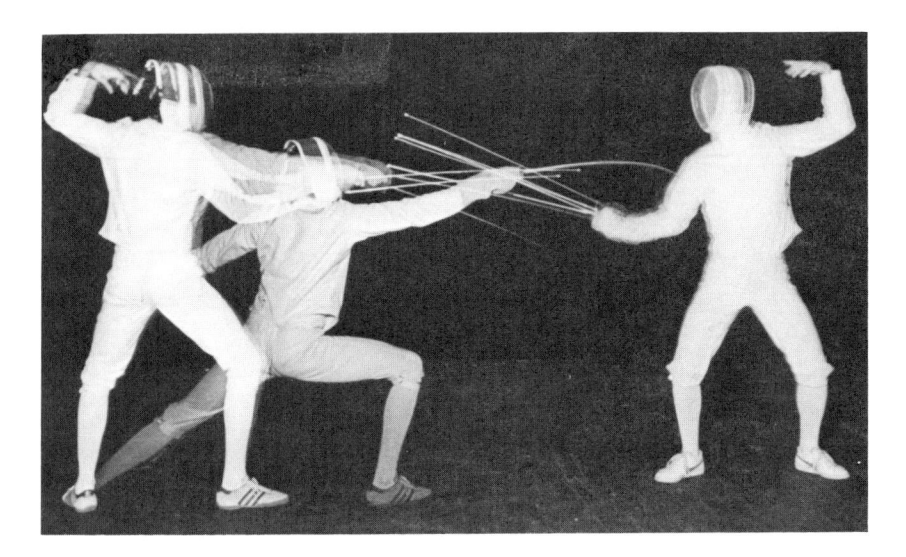

4.17 The One-Two-Three Attack (Double Disengage)

4.18 The Beat Attack

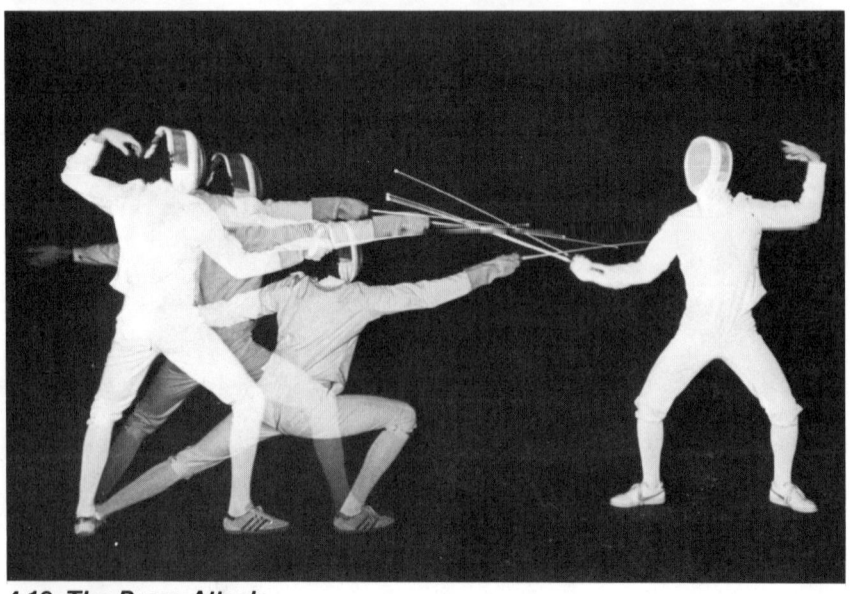

4.19 The Press Attack

Attacks on the Blade

Attacks on the blade are any movements with the specific purpose of moving the blade out of line as the attack is initiated so that a line is open for the attack, or so the opponent is unable to free his/her blade to defend against the attack.

The Beat Attack

The beat is executed by making a sharp rap with the midsection of one's blade on the foible or midsection of the opponent's blade with the specific purpose of opening a line for attack. Immediately following the sharp rap, a rapid thrust followed by a lunge concludes the attack (*Fig. 4.18*).

The Press Attack

The results of the press attack are very much like those of the beat; however, the action is much more subtle in an effort to make it difficult for the opponent to detect or analyze what is happening. The press is executed by the attacking fencer pressing forcefully on the opponent's blade in order to open a line (*Fig. 4.19*). It is important that the attacking fencer remember to keep the point in line. Therefore, the pressing action must be done with either a slight abduction or adduction of the foil hand, depending on which line the attack is occurring. Quite often as one's opponent feels the pressure on their blade, the immediate reaction is to return pressure. If this happens, the attacking fencer might want to consider leaving the opponent's blade, executing a rapid disengage and going in on the opposite line. Thus, for variety, another attack has been added—the press disengage attack.

The Glide Attack

The glide attack is an attack along the blade in which the attacking fencer traps and controls the foible of the opponent's blade between the bell guard and forte of his/her own blade. Gradual pressure is applied to the blade as the attacker extends, slides along the opponent's blade, and lands (*Fig. 4.20a-c*). The purpose of this attack is to open a line with the pressure and to keep an awareness of the opponent's blade by maintaining contact throughout the offensive action. As in any attack, effectiveness is greatly dependent on the speed and control with which it is executed.

The Bind

The bind is an attack on the blade. If done properly, it can disarm the opponent. This attack is most effective when used against the extended foil arm of an opponent. As one begins to execute the bind, the extended arm

54 THE FENCING BOOK

4.20a The Glide Attack

4.20b The Glide Attack

IV. BLADE ACTIONS 55

4.20c The Glide Attack

of the attacker should move out and quickly over the opponent's blade. The mechanical relationship of the blade puts the attacker's forte on and riding over the foible and midsection of the opponent's blade. The bind is an attack that carries the blade on a diagonal from a high line to a low line. Therefore, if the attack begins in the high inside line, the attempt to score would be made in the low outside line. Conversely, if the attack was initiated in the high outside line, the attempt to land would be in the low inside line. When executing the bind, beginning in the high inside line, as the proper mechanical relationship of the blades is achieved, there should be a rapid pronation of the foil hand as the blade moves over the opponent's extended blade (*Fig. 4.21a-d*). This pronation of the foil hand also puts the blade in a proper position to hit and stick in the low outside line. If the bind attack is initiated in the high outside line, as one controls the opponent's foible with the forte of the blade, the rapid supination of the attacking blade not only controls the opponent's blade, but puts the hand in the proper position for hitting and sticking in the low inside line. When two left-handed fencers are fencing each other, the above techniques also apply. However, when a left-handed fencer is fencing a right-handed one or vice versa, the mechanics of the foil hand must be reversed.

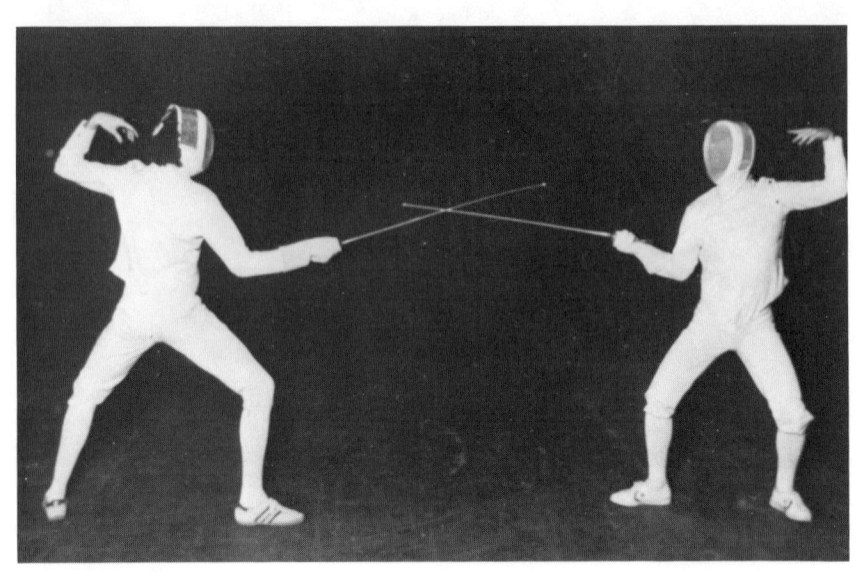

4.21a The Bind

4.21b The Bind

IV. BLADE ACTIONS 57

4.21c The Bind

4.21d The Bind

The Envelopment

The envelopment has many of the same qualities as the bind. The attack is initiated in much the same way. However, instead of moving on a diagonal through just three lines, it moves through all four lines of attack and lands in the line of original engagement. When executing the envelopment, one attempts to establish the mechanical relationship of having the forte of the attacking blade control the foible of the defending blade. If the envelopment is started in the high inside line, the initial contact is made, forte to foible, the hand is pronated rapidly and rotated through the four lines of the opponent's target area, bringing the attacking foil back into the line of original engagement. As one moves to conclude the attack with a lunge, the foil hand should be quickly supinated. To begin the envelopment, the attacking arm should be extended and threatening. Every effort should be made to keep the attacking point as close to the opponent's bell guard as possible. As the point moves into the original line of engagement, it is followed by a very rapid lunge (*Fig. 4.22a-e*). The envelopment can be initiated in any of the four lines—high outside, high inside, low outside, and low inside—and executed effectively as long as the mechanical relationship between the attacking blade and the defending blade is consistent.

Derobement

Derobement is also referred to as the ability to deceive an opponent's attempt to engage, beat, or bind the blade. As one's opponent attempts to take the blade, the attacker drops the point just low enough for the parry to pass over the blade and then attacks.

ADVANCED TECHNIQUES

The following are just a few of the many available advanced techniques one can use to improve their game and challenge opponents.

The Double

The double is used when an opponent uses a counter parry instead of a direct parry against a feint disengage. The attacker deceives the counter parry by continuing in a circle around the parry. In this particular blade action, there is no change of direction as the point disengages. The point continues in the same direction as it began until it completes one and one-half circles and lands in the line first threatened by the feint. The double is a beautiful blade action but it is dependent solely on one's opponent using a counter parry instead of a lateral parry for defense.

IV. BLADE ACTIONS

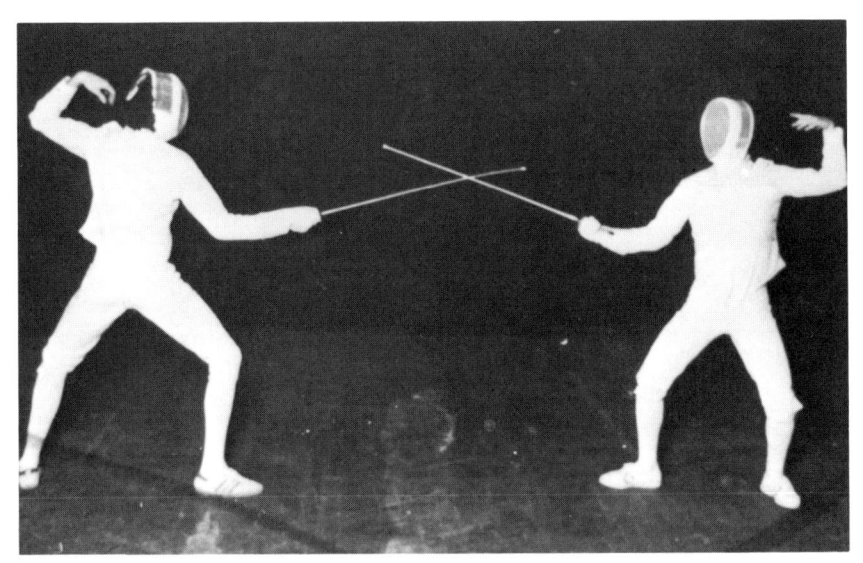

4.22a The Envelopment

4.22b The Envelopment

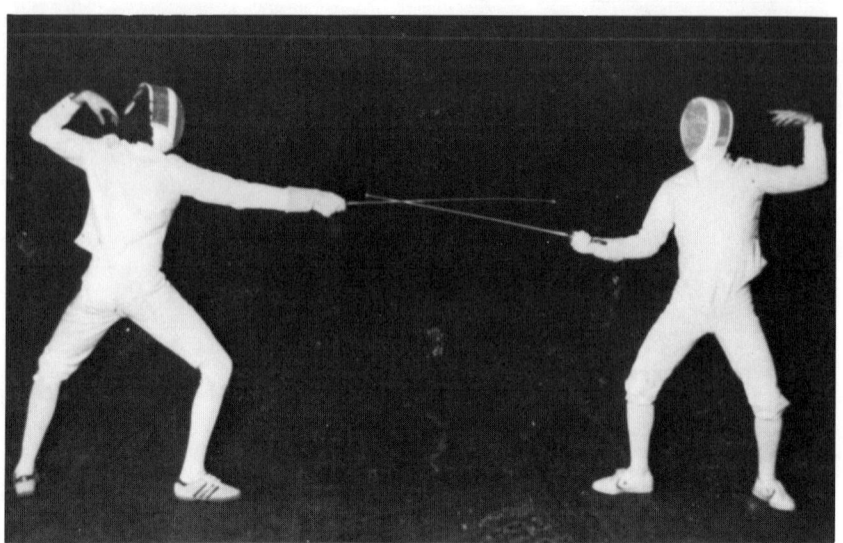

4.22c *The Envelopment*

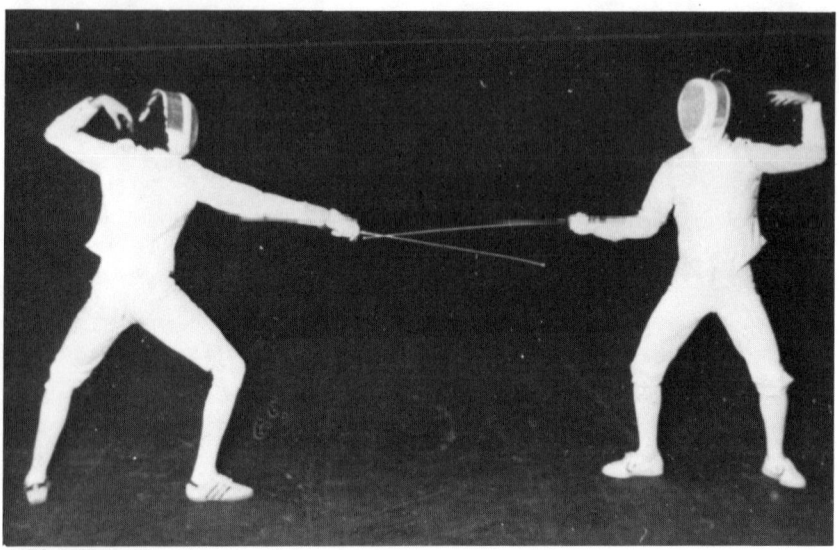

4.22d *The Envelopment*

IV. BLADE ACTIONS   61

4.22e The Envelopment

Passata-sotto

The passata-sotto is most easily described as simply ducking under an opponent's attack or displacing one's body beneath the attack while impaling the attacker with a thrust (*Fig. 4.23*). The thrust is made with the hand in a pronated position. The front foot of the fencer remains stationary while the back leg is extended and slides backward. The forward knee is flexed more than it would normally be in a traditional lunge and the non-foil hand touches the floor beside the forward foot in order to support the fencer. The element of surprise is crucial in determining the effectiveness of the attack.

Inquartata

The inquartata is a technique that gets its name for its quarter side-step backward which removes the defendant's target area from the line of attack, and thus enables him/her to dodge a possible scoring touch. As one's opponent extends with a thrust and lunge attack, the defender simply lifts their rear foot and displaces it to the side and backward approximately 18 inches and leans away from the attacking blade. After removing the target from the threatening attack, the fencer quickly extends to the closest open area of the attacker and lands. This dodging movement and the extension of the point in line must be done simultaneously, thus forcing the attacker to impale themselves on the blade (*Fig. 4.24*).

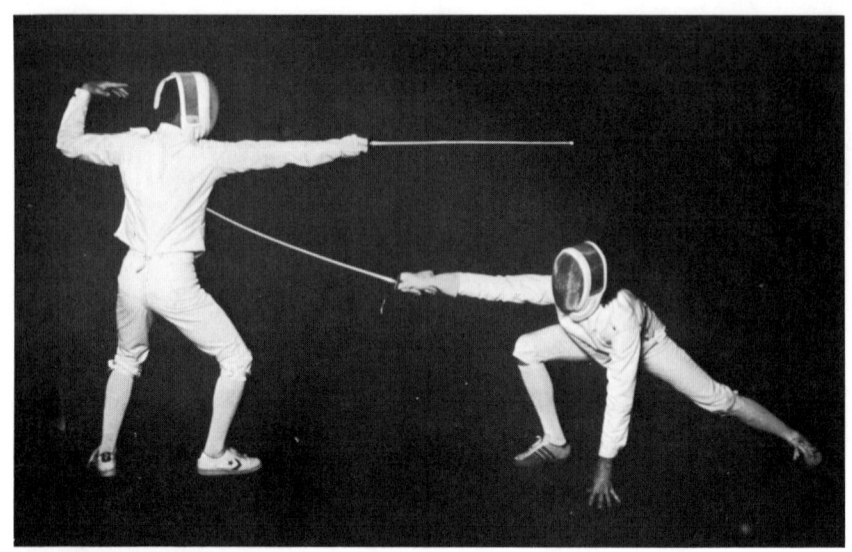

4.23 Passata-Sotto

4.24 Inquartata

The Remise

The remise is an immediate second effort of an attack done without withdrawing the arm. This effort is made in the same line as the original attack. The remise is used exclusively against the defender who delays the riposte or continually uses extensive compound blade actions as a counter attack.

The Redoublement

The redoublement is an immediate second effort of an attack done without withdrawing the arm. This effort is made in a new line because the initial line of the attack is still closed. The redoublement is quite often used against an opponent who does not riposte following a parry.

The Reprise

The reprise consists of retaking an attack against an opponent who cannot be reached with continual or repeated lunges. It is usually associated with a recovery forward so the distance between the fencers can be covered on the retaking effort. The reprise is usually executed with an advanced lunge in order to land.

DEFENSIVE BLADE ACTIONS

Defensive actions in fencing consist primarily of parries. A parry may be executed by beating the opponent's blade sharply or more subtly by applying continuous pressure to the attacking blade. The desired result is to move the attacking blade out of line. Historically, there were eight original parries. They were named and numbered consecutively, one through eight, with parry one being the first possible defensive movement one could make after drawing the weapon from a sword belt. Progressing through the other parries, one can note the definite aim of getting the blade up so counter attacks could be made to the torso. The cavalier in the figures illustrates what could happen when attacked by an adversary. He draws his weapon to protect himself. The first possible defensive movement is parry one (Fig. 4.25). The second defensive movement he could possibly make is parry two (Fig. 4.26). Parried, the adversary tries again. The third defensive movement is parry three (Fig. 4.27). The sequence of attacks in parries continues for parry four (Fig. 4.28), five (Fig. 4.29), six (Fig. 4.30), seven (Fig. 4.31), and eight (Fig. 4.32). These eight defensive movements are the eight parries known to the sport of fencing today.

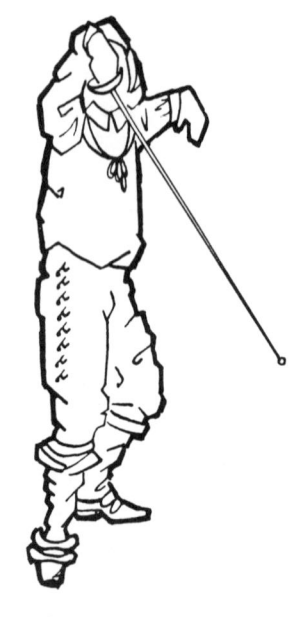

64   THE FENCING BOOK

4.25 Parry 1

4.26 Parry 2

4.27 Parry 3

4.28 Parry 4

IV. BLADE ACTIONS 65

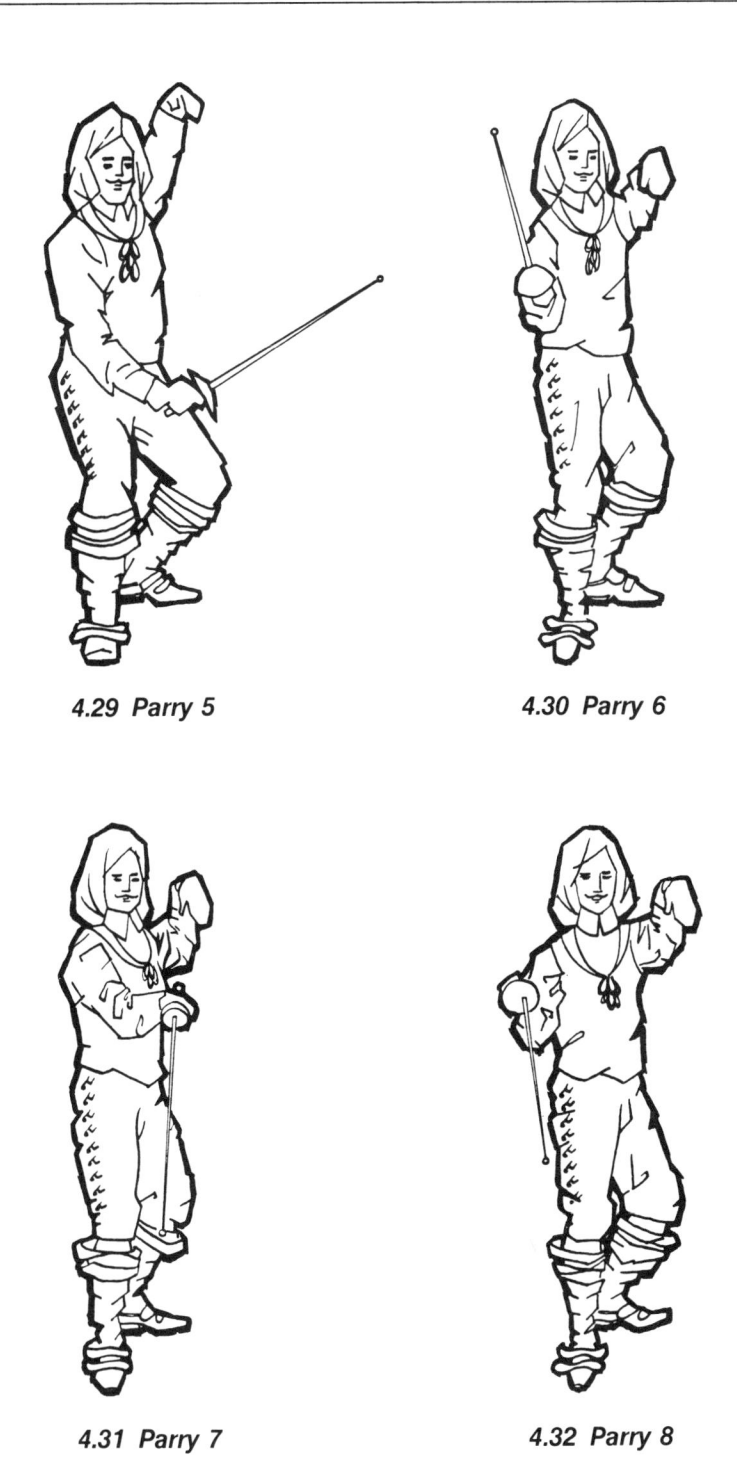

4.29 Parry 5

4.30 Parry 6

4.31 Parry 7

4.32 Parry 8

66 THE FENCING BOOK

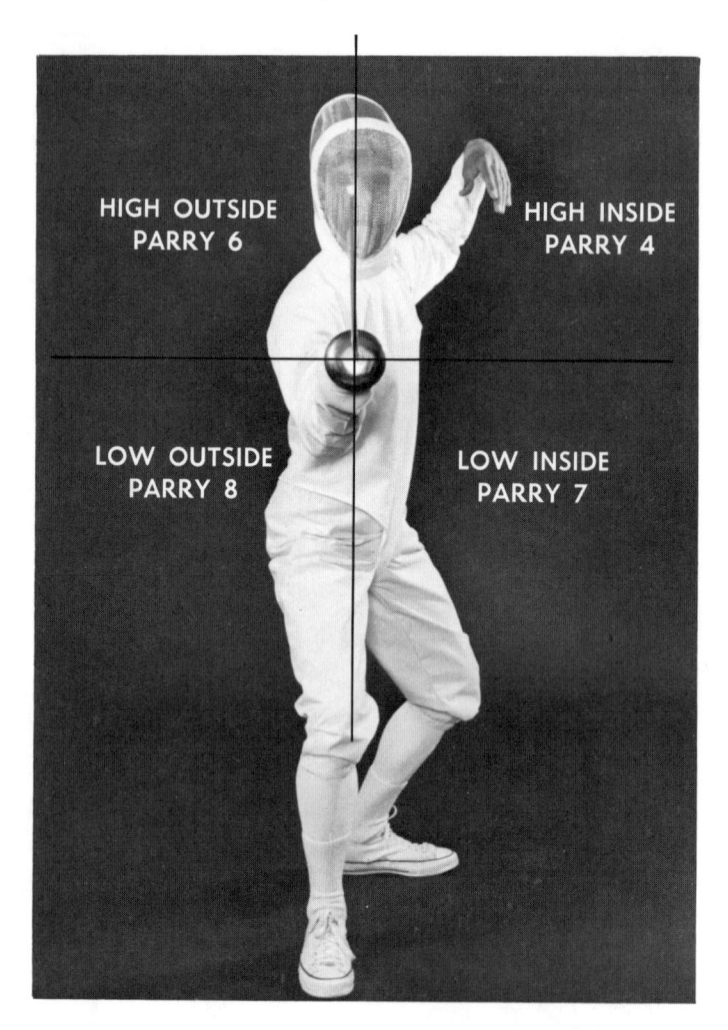

HIGH OUTSIDE
PARRY 6

HIGH INSIDE
PARRY 4

LOW OUTSIDE
PARRY 8

LOW INSIDE
PARRY 7

4.33 Lines of Attack and Parries That Defend Them

Although it is important for a fencer to have knowledge of all eight traditional parries, seldom, if ever, will more than four in the rapid-paced, modern-day fencing be used. The parries most often used to defend the four lines of attack are 4, 6, 7, and 8 (*Fig. 4.33*).

In all parries, whether high line or low line, the effectiveness is largely determined by the proper mechanical relationship to the opponent's attacking blade. It has been stated that parallel lines will never meet except, perhaps, in infinity. For this reason, the parrying blade should have a definite angle with respect to the attacking blade. The proper mechanical relationship dictates that the defender control the foible of the attacking blade with

IV. BLADE ACTIONS

the forte of the defending blade. During the parry, the defending fencer should keep the foil point on target so if he/she desires to riposte, the foil point will be in line with the opponent's target. Another important concept to remember in executing parries is to displace the opponent's attacking blade sideways regardless of whether the attack is in the high line or the low line. If a defender attempts to displace the blade either up or down, a hit on an invalid surface may result.

Parry 4

In order to execute an effective parry four, the fencer adducts the foil arm at the shoulder horizontally and hyperextends the wrist of the foil arm (*Fig. 4.34*). By making and maintaining contact on the attacking blade with the forte of the blade, the defending fencer is able to carry the attacking blade out of line and away from a valid target area (*Fig. 4.35*). The hyperextension of the wrist allows for an effective parry and also for the defending foil point to remain in line for a quick counter-attack. When one grips the foil in the guard position, the normal position is with the hand slightly supinated and the thumb of the foil hand for right-handed fencers being at the one o'clock position. During the execution of parry 4 as the foil arm is adducted approximately four to six inches horizontally, the foil hand should pronate slightly so that the thumb moves from the one o'clock position to approximately the 11 o'clock position (*Fig. 4.36*). These references should be reversed for a left-handed fencer, who should begin with the thumb of the foil hand at 11 o'clock and pronate it to a position of one o'clock.

Parry 6

By abducting the foil arm approximately four inches to six inches horizontally at the shoulder and supinating the foil hand, the fencer is able to execute a parry 6 effectively (*Fig. 4.37*). As one supinates the hand there is a slight wrist flexion which pulls the pommel on top of the wrist. The fencer makes contact with the attacking blade with the forte of his own blade and carries it away from the line of intent (*Fig. 4.38*). The foil hand of the defending fencer starts with the thumb in the one o'clock position. As the fencer abducts the foil arm and supinates the hand, the thumb should rotate to a three o'clock position (*Fig. 4.39*). This rotation is coupled with a slight ulnar flexion to insure that the point of the defending blade remains in line for a riposte. Parry 6 sometimes feels a bit awkward simply because at its completion, the wrist of the foil hand should be abducted to a position slightly outside the elbow of the foil arm. The above references should be reversed for a left-handed fencer, who should begin with the thumb at eleven o'clock and supinate it to nine o'clock.

4.34 Parry 4 (Solo)

IV. BLADE ACTIONS 69

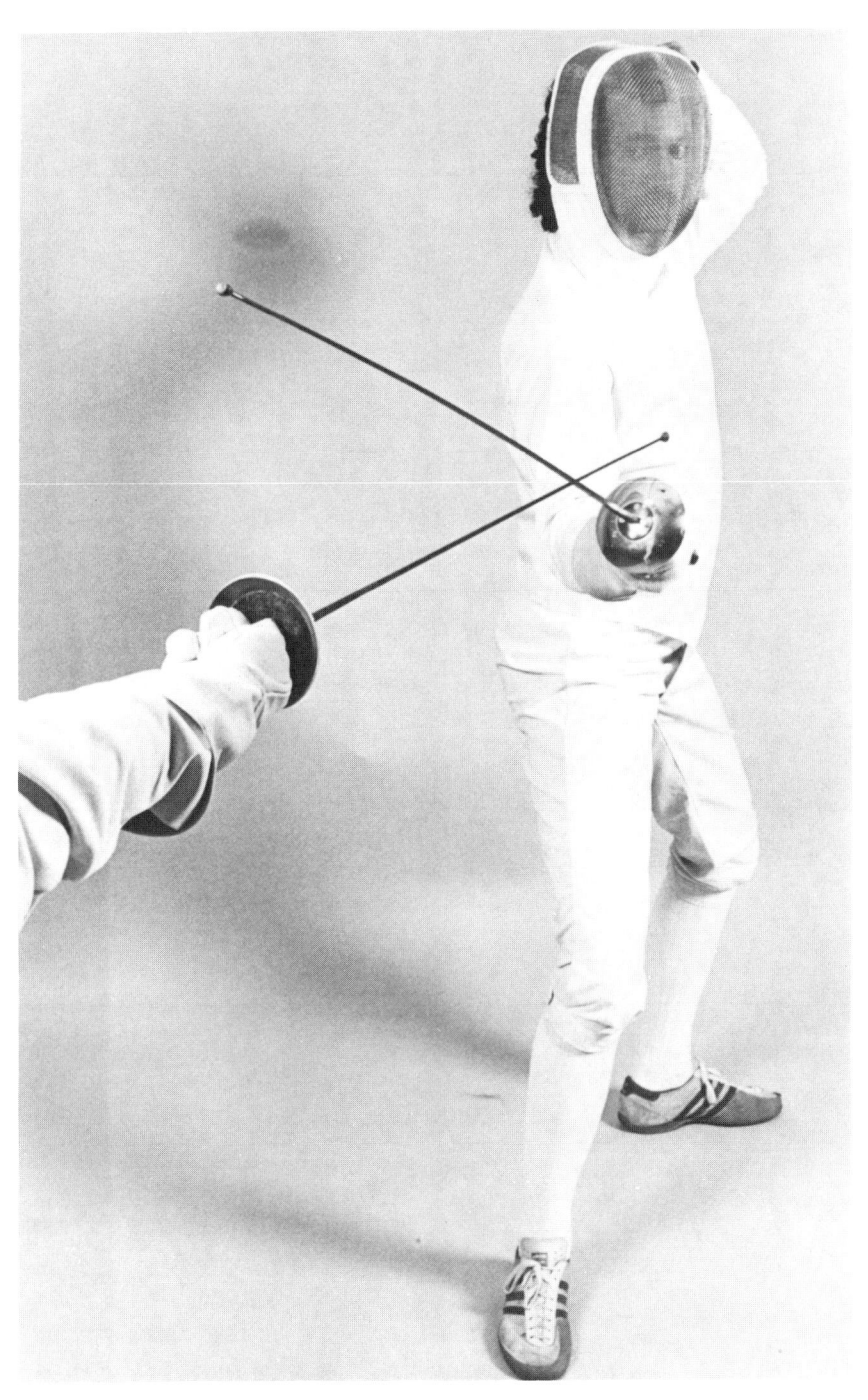

4.35 Parry 4 with Attack

4.36 Parry 4 Overhead

IV. BLADE ACTIONS 71

4.37 Parry 6 (Solo)

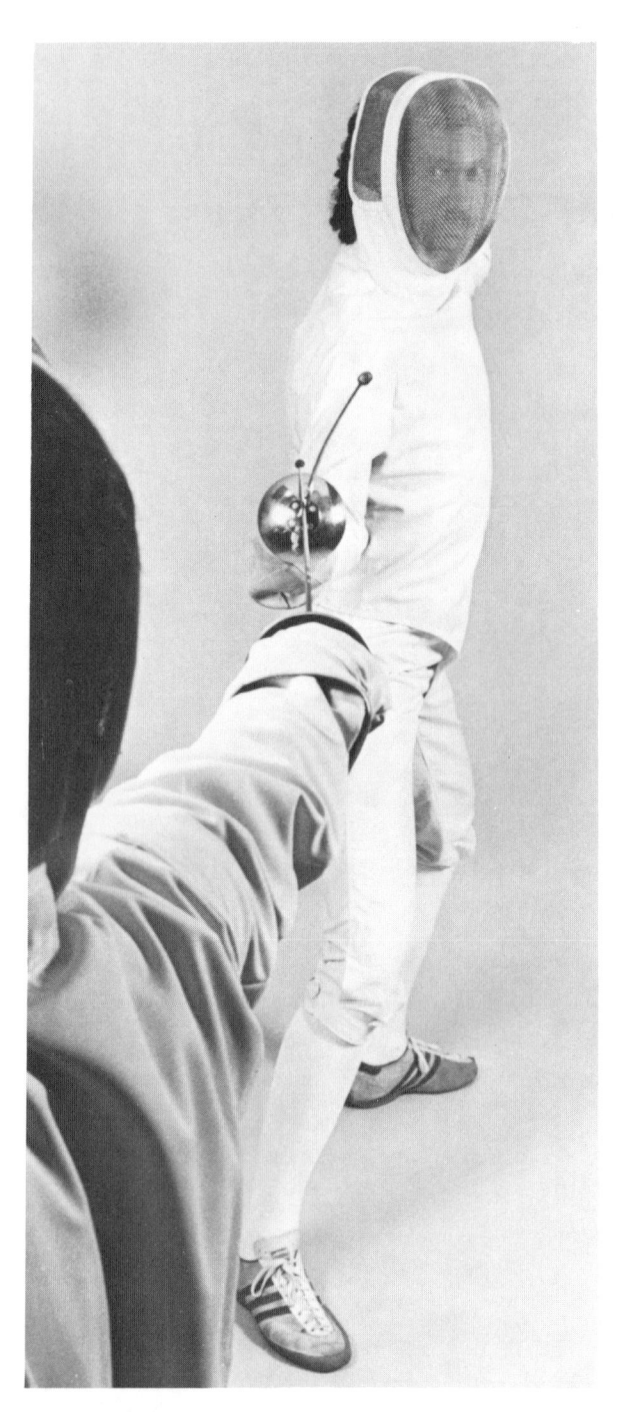

4.38 Parry 6 with Attack

IV. BLADE ACTIONS 73

4.39 Parry 6 Overhead

Parry 7

Parry 7 is used to defend the low inside line. In order to defend that line effectively, a fencer drops their foil point to a position below the bell guard of the attacking blade (*Fig. 4.40*). He/she supinates the foil hand slightly and the foil arm horizontally adducts at the shoulder approximately four to six inches, with the result that the attacking foible is trapped by the defending forte and pushed from its line of intent (*Fig. 4.41*). The hand position for parry 7 should start with the thumb in the one o'clock position. As the attacking blade is trapped with the forte of the defending blade and moved to the side, the defending fencer's hand is supinated even further so the thumb is approximately at three o'clock (*Fig. 4.42*). Again, this action should be reversed for a left-handed fencer, who begins with the thumb at eleven o'clock and rotates it to nine o'clock.

Parry 8

Parry 8 is used to protect the low outside line. In executing parry 8, a fencer supinates the foil hand, placing the point below the bell guard of the attacking blade (*Fig. 4.43*). As the attacking blade comes in, the defending fencer traps the foible of the attacking blade with the forte of the defending blade (*Fig. 4.44*). The defender then abducts the foil arm horizontally at the shoulder approximately four to six inches and supinates the foil hand from the one o'clock to the three o'clock position, carrying the blade out of the line of intent (*Fig. 4.45*). This action is reversed for the left-handed fencer, who should begin with the thumb in the eleven o'clock position and further supinate it to the nine o'clock position.

Parries one, two, three, four, five, six, seven, and eight are often referred to as direct parries. In addition to those eight, there are semi-circular parries or counter parries.

Semi-circular Parries

In executing a semi-circular parry, the point of the defending weapon describes a small, sweeping arch or semi-circular movement as the blade moves from a high line to a low line or vice versa.

Circular Parries

Circular or counter parries, as they are sometimes called, are made by changing lines with a very small circular motion of the blade and following that movement by a direct parry. For example, if an attack is made to the high outside line, the defending fencer may choose to disengage and use a direct parry 4. This entire movement would be called a counter 4 parry. If an attack were made in the high inside line, the defending fencer might elect to

IV. BLADE ACTIONS

4.40 Parry 7 (Solo)

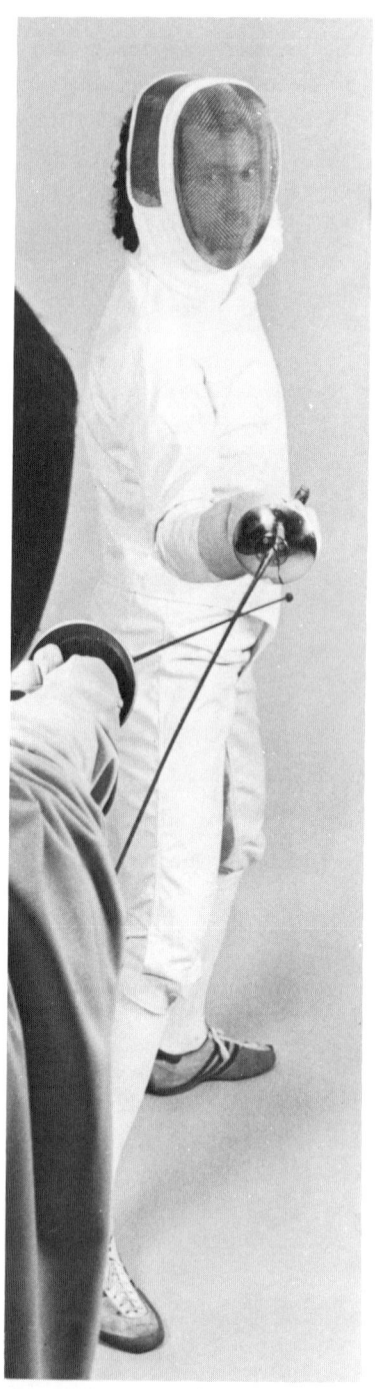

4.41 Parry 7 with Attack

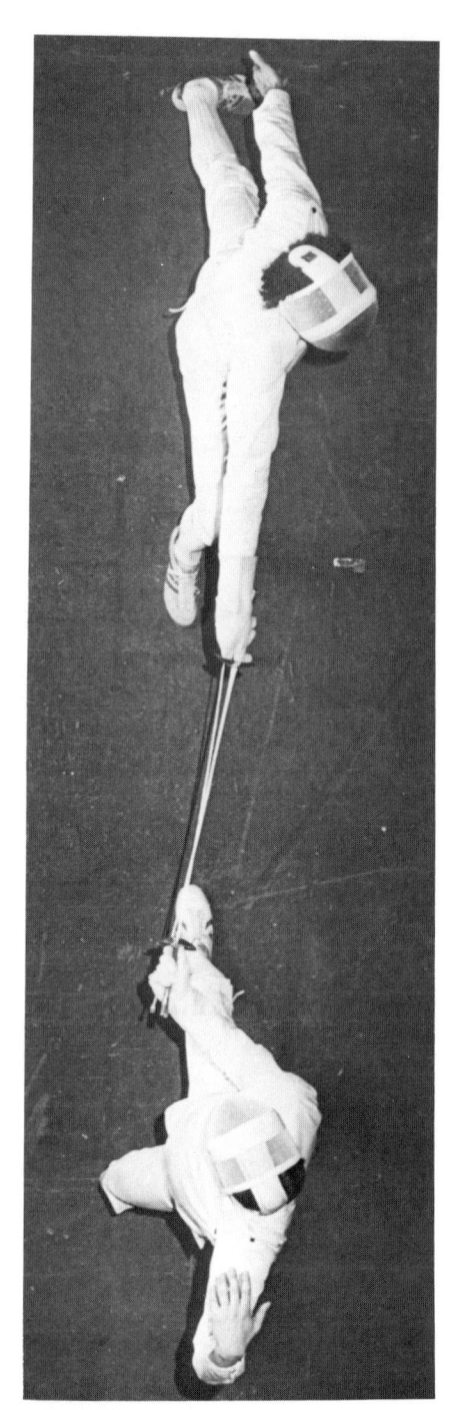

4.42 Parry 7 Overhead

IV. BLADE ACTIONS 77

4.43 Parry 8 (Solo)

4.44 Parry 8 with Attack

IV. BLADE ACTIONS   79

4.45 Parry 8 Overhead

disengage and use a parry 6. This movement would be referred to as a counter 6 (*Fig. 4.46a-c*).

Beginning fencers quite often find the counter or circular parries to be tedious and somewhat slow; however, time should be taken to improve these skills. It is importnat that all fencers be able to execute both direct parries, semi-circular parries, and counter parries effectively in order to add variation to their style of defense.

The Riposte

A riposte may be defined as a return following a successful parry. The fencer who has effectively defended themselves may choose to strike back with riposte. It is an excellent training experience for a fencer to be taught to riposte with all parries. Best results can be obtained if the riposte is initiated without hesitation immediately following a parry. When executing a riposte, the fencer should make every attempt to get in and score on the shortest, fastest possible route. Therefore, a direct thrust is quite often the most effective riposte (*Fig. 4.47a-c*). A counter riposte may be executed in much the same way as the riposte; however, this is done by a fencer who has successfully parried a riposte. By continuing the riposte or counter riposte, we find the fencers moving into a conversation of blades.

Strategy against the Bind

The most practical defense against the bind is the movement of the defending blade to a low line parry (seven or eight), depending, of course, in which line the attack was initiated. Many times a defending fencer will opt for parries one or two due to the added power he/she feels can be employed. However, it depends in which of the lines the attacker initiates the action.

If the attacker is in some way telegraphing a plan to use the bind and the defender can get the message, a simple defense would be to derobe and prevent the attacker from taking the blade.

Another ploy for effective defense is retreating one step with each attack from the opponent. Following that retreat, the fencer should immediately attempt to regain the ground lost, or be in danger of being pushed back to the warning line of the piste.

Defense against the Envelopment

The defense against the envelopment is similar to that of the bind, using low line defenses of parries seven, eight, one, or two. However, parries four and six can also be employed as effective defenses because the attacking blade will at times be in the high lines.

IV. BLADE ACTIONS 81

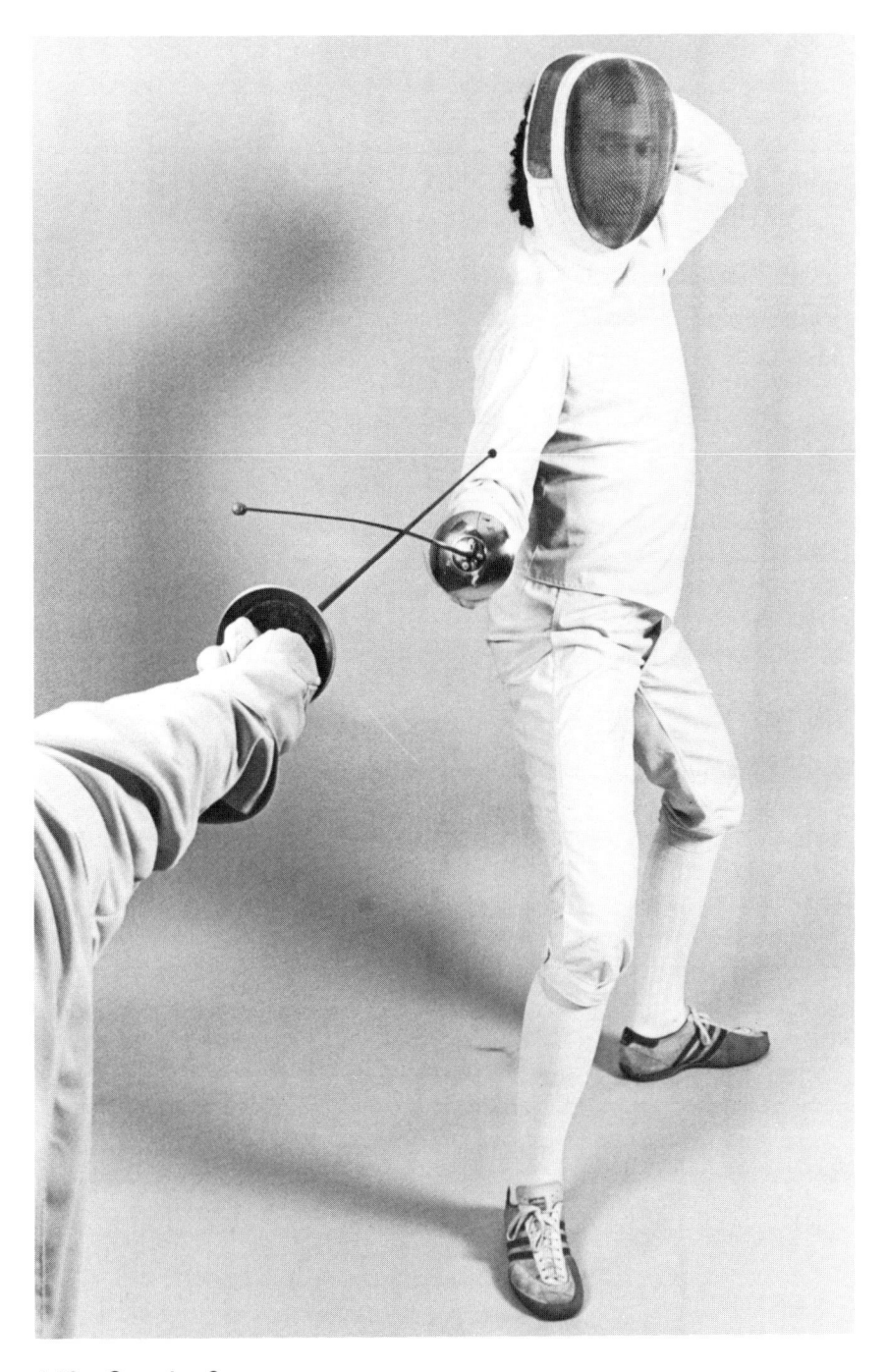

4.46a Counter 6

4.46b Counter 6

IV. BLADE ACTIONS 83

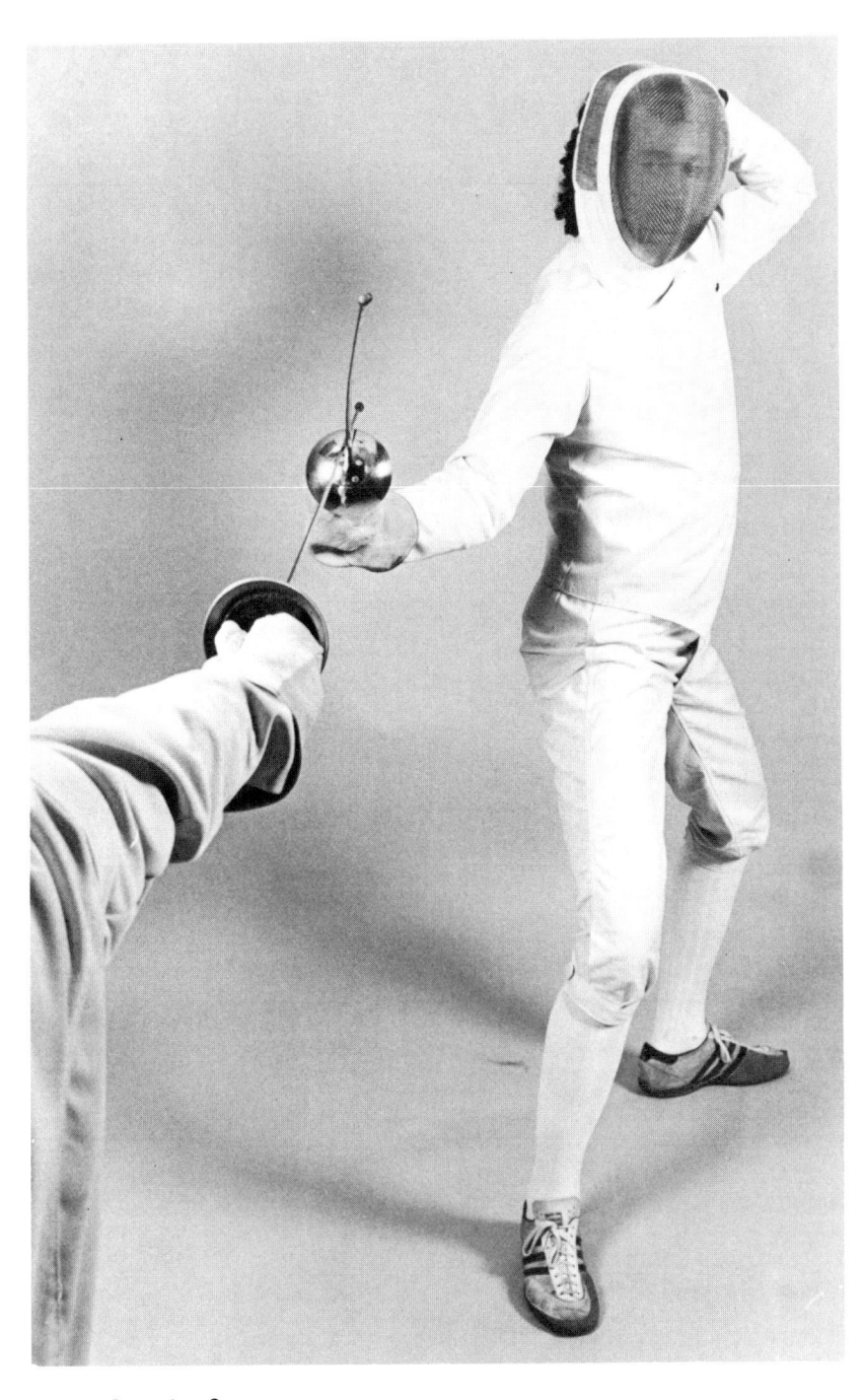

4.46c Counter 6

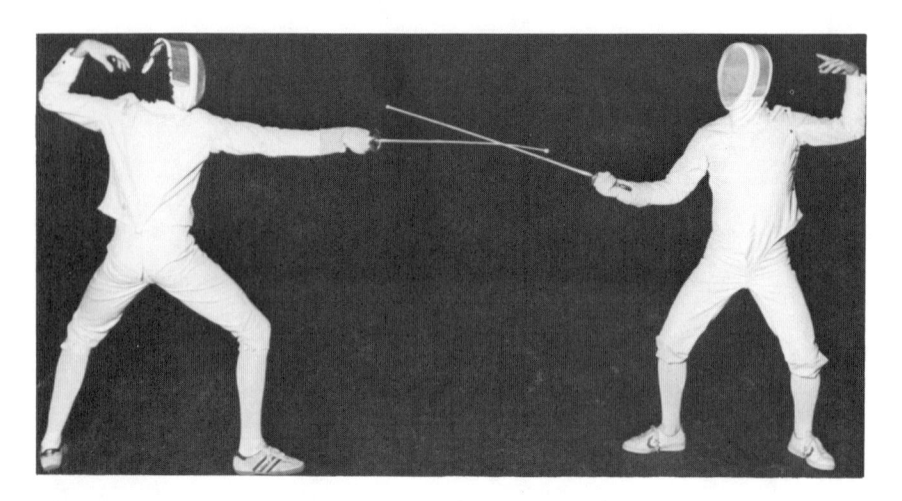

4.47a Attack

4.47b Parry

COUNTER ATTACKS

Counter attacks are offensive actions made against the attacks of one's opponent.

The Stop Thrust

The stop thrust is a counter attack made during a hesitation or delay in an attack. In order to count as a valid touch, the stop thrust must land before the opponent's final movement begins.

IV. BLADE ACTIONS   85

4.47c Riposte

A stop thrust is most useful when an attacker executes a faulty attack in which there is a definite withdrawal of the foil arm; or the attack is not in line and fails to threaten the target. The fencer who executes the stop thrust need not parry, but simply extends, keeping the point in line, and allows the opponent to impale themself on the blade. The inquartata and the passata-sotto are excellent tactics to use in this endeavor.

The Time Thrust

The time thrust is a counter attack made into the opponent's blade, serving as both a parry and riposte. The effectiveness of this action is dependent on the fencer's ability to determine the line in which the opponent's attack will come.

Evaluation Questions

1. What are the two types of attacks used in fencing?
2. What determines the effectiveness of a parry?
3. What is right-of-way?
4. What is a riposte?
5. When must a riposte be executed in order to be effective?
6. How many different compound attacks can you design with the skills you have learned?

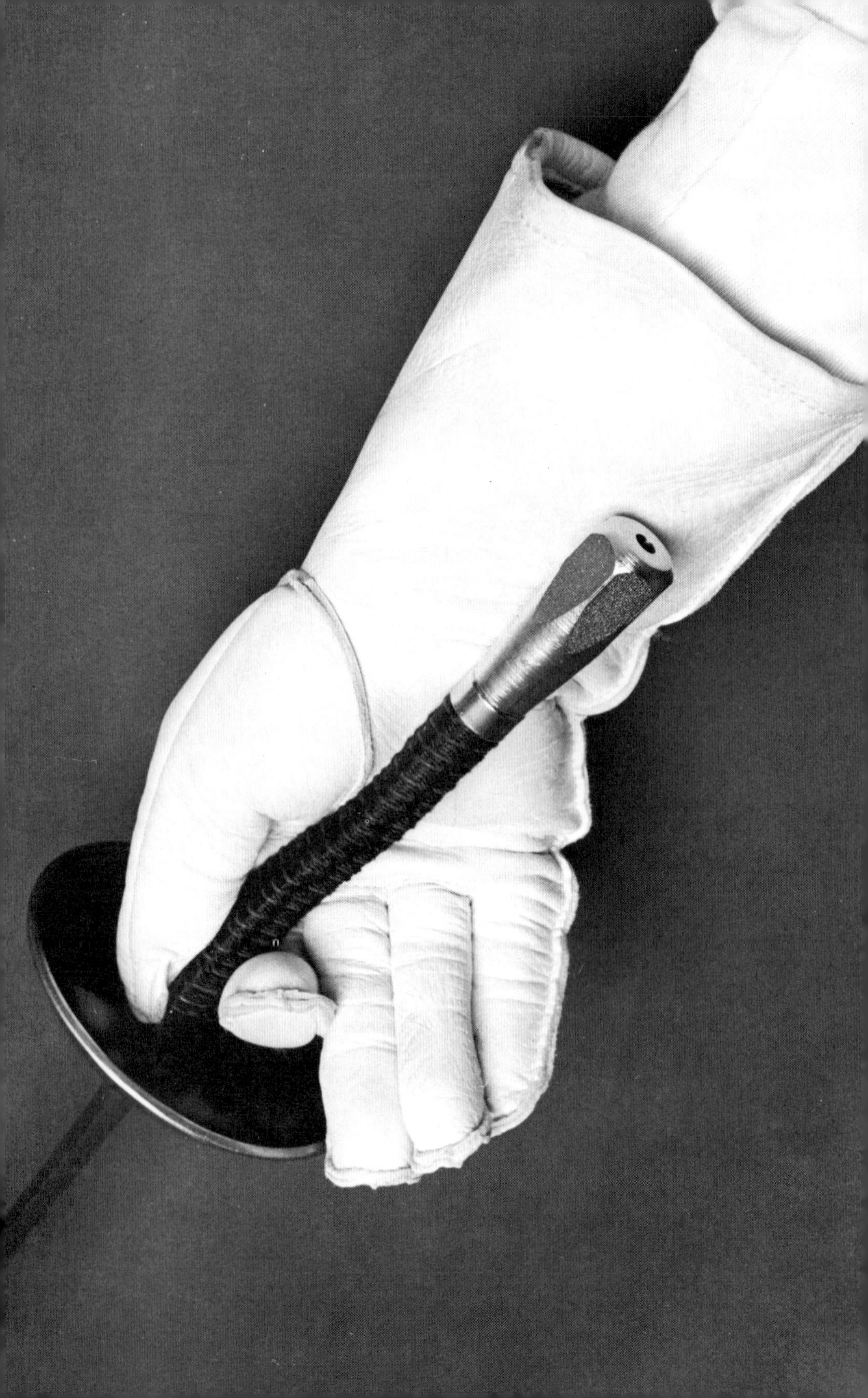

CHAPTER FIVE

Rules of Play

The rules of fencing in the United States are published by the United States Fencing Association. The USFA works under the auspices of the Federation Internationale d'Escrime (FIE), which governs world fencing. The rules of play printed in the following pages have been taken from the USFA rule book, with permission of the Association. The system of notation reproduced is that of the manual itself.

All fencers are strongly encouraged to purchase the USFA Rules Book.

TERMINOLOGY

A. DIRECTOR [PRESIDENT OF THE JURY]
3   Throughout the text of the present rules, the word *Director* will be used to mean "Director of Combat" or "Président de Jury" [the latter is the French term used internationally].

B. COMPETITIONS
Sec. 1. *Free play and bout*
4   Friendly combat between two fencers is called "free play" ["assault"]; when the score is kept in a competition, it is called a "bout" ["match"].
Sec. 2. *Team match*
5   The total of bouts between the fencers of two different teams is called a "match" ["rencontre"].
Sec. 3. *Competition*
6   A competition is the aggregate of the bouts (in an individual competition) or of the team matches (in a team competition) necessary to determine the winner of the competition ["épreuve"].

Competitions are classified according to the weapons, the sex of the competitors, or their age, or their occupation (members of the armed forces, students, etc.), and by whether they are competitions for individuals or for teams.

Competitions are said to be "by direct elimination" when the competitors are eliminated upon their first loss (or after their second if the rules provide for a repechage table); a "pool" ["poule"], on the other hand, is a group of several competitors (or of all the competitors) who all fence each other successively to determine their respective classification.

Sec. 4. *Championship*

7   Championship ["championnat"] is the name given to a competition held to ascertain the best fencer or the best team in each weapon, within a sports organization, in a given area, and for a set period of time.

Sec. 5. *Tournament*

8   Tournament ["tournoi"] is the name given to the whole of the competitions held at the same place, in the same period of time, and on the same occasion.

C. EXPLANATION OF CERTAIN TECHNICAL TERMS MOST OFTEN USED IN JUDGING FENCING.

Sec. 1. *Fencing time*

9   Fencing time [or: period of fencing time; "Temps d'escrime"] is the time required to perform one simple fencing action.

Sec. 2. *Offensive and defensive actions*

10   The different offensive actions are the attack, the riposte, and the counter-riposte.

The *attack* is the initial offensive action executed by extending the arm and continuously threatening the opponent's valid surface [target].

The *riposte* is the offensive action made by the fencer who has parried the attack.

The *counter-riposte* is the offensive action made by the fencer who has parried the riposte.

The different defensive actions are the parries.

The *parry* ["parade"] is the defensive action made with the weapon to prevent the attack from touching.

Parries are *simple,* or direct, when they are made in the same line as the attack.

They are *circular* (counter) when they are executed in the line opposite to that of the attack.

11   *Offensive Actions:*

a) *Attack or riposte*

The action is *simple* when it is executed in a single movement;

either *direct* (in the same line),

or *indirect* (in another line).

The action is *composite* when it is executed in several movements.

b. *Riposte*

The riposte is *immediate* or *delayed* ["a temps perdu"]; this is a question of fact [what action is performed] and of the speed of execution.

V. RULES OF PLAY

Examples:
1. Simple direct ripostes:

Direct [straight] riposte: a riposte which touches the opponent without having left the line in which the parry was made.

Riposte along the blade: a riposte which touches the opponent by gliding along the blade after the parry.

2. Simple indirect ripostes:

Riposte by disengagement: a riposte which touches the opponent in the line opposite to that in which the parry was made (by passing beneath the blade, if the parry was in the high line, and over the blade, if the parry was in the low line).

Riposte by coupé [cutover]: a riposte which touches the opponent in the line opposite to that in which the parry was made (in all cases, by passing the blade over the opponent's point).

3. Composite ripostes:

Riposte with a double: a riposte which touches the opponent in the line opposite to that in which the parry was made, but after having described a full circle around the opponent's blade.

Riposte by one-two: a riposte which touches the opponent in the line in which the parry was made, but after having first been in the opposite line, by passing under the opponent's blade.

And so forth.

Sec. 3. *Counter attacks*

12 Counter attacks are offensive or defensive-offensive actions executed during the opponent's attack:

a) The *Stop* [stop thrust or cut]: is a counter attack made on an attack.

b) The *Stop with opposition* (formerly called the "time thrust" or "time hit"): is a counter attack executed while closing the line in which the opponent's attack will be terminated.

c) The *Stop in time:* is made with a period of fencing time.

Sec. 4. *Kinds of offensive actions*

13 a) *Remise*

The remise is an immediate simple offensive action which follows an original action; it is made without withdrawing the arm, after the opponent's parry or retreat, either because the latter gives up contact with the blade without riposting, or delays his riposte, or attempts an indirect or composite riposte.

b) *Redoublement*

The redoublement is a new action, either simple or composite, made against an opponent who has parried without riposting, or has simply evaded the first action by a retreat or a displacement.

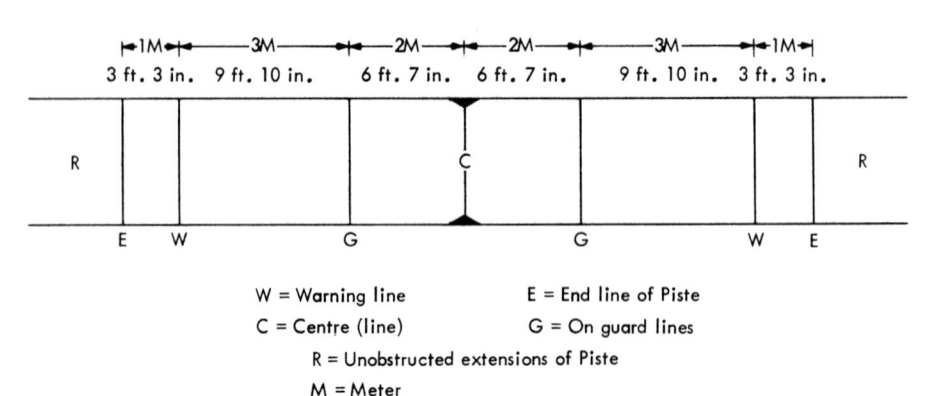

THE REGULATION PISTE FOR FOIL FENCING

|←1M→|←——3M——→|←—2M—→|←—2M—→|←——3M——→|←1M→|
3 ft. 3 in. 9 ft. 10 in. 6 ft. 7 in. 6 ft. 7 in. 9 ft. 10 in. 3 ft. 3 in.

R   C   R

E   W   G   G   W   E

W = Warning line   E = End line of Piste
C = Centre (line)   G = On guard lines
R = Unobstructed extensions of Piste
M = Meter

5.1 The Strip

c) *Reprise d'attaque* [retaking of the attack]
The reprise is a new attack executed immediately after a return to the guard position.

d) *Counter time*
Counter time describes every action made by an attacker against the opponent's stop.

FIELD OF PLAY ["TERRAIN"]

14   The field of play must present an even surface. It may not offer either an advantage or a disadvantage to either of the two competitors, particularly as regards gradient or light.

In announcing a tournament, the organizers must always specify the type of surface on which the events will be fenced. They must be especially specific when the events will be fenced in the open air.

15   The portion of the field of play used for fencing is called the strip ["piste"]. The strip may be of earth, wood, linoleum, cork, rubber, plastic, metal, metallic mesh, or of a material with a metallic base.

The width of the strip is from 1.8 to 2 meters; its length varies according to the weapon.

Besides the length specified for each weapon, the strip should be extended at each end by 1.5 to 2 meters, to allow the fencer who is going to cross the rear limit to retreat over an even and unbroken surface.

If the strip is placed on a platform, the latter may not be more than 0.5 meter high.

V. RULES OF PLAY

If, for practical reasons, the strip cannot be regulation length, its length may not in any case be less than 13 meters, including the extensions mentioned above (*Fig. 5.1*).

FENCERS' EQUIPMENT
(WEAPONS—OTHER EQUIPMENT—CLOTHING)

Sec. 1 *Responsibility of fencers*

16   Fencers arm, equip and clothe themselves and fence on their own responsibility and at their own risk and peril.

Fencers alone may be held responsible in all respects for accidents in which they figure as agents or as victims.

The safety precautions as well as the inspection procedures specified in these rules are intended only to improve the safety of the fencers, and cannot guarantee it absolutely. Consequently, whatever may be the manner in which they are applied, they cannot entail liability on the part of the FIE, or of the organizers of a competition, or of the officials in charge of the latter, or of those who may cause an accident.

Sec. 2. *Inspection ["Controle"] of fencers' equipment*

17   Fencers are responsible for the condition of their gear (weapon and other equipment and clothing) at the moment they appear on the strip.

The inspection procedures prescribed by the present rules are intended only to assist the organizers who must enforce the rules and the fencers who must abide by the rules. Accordingly, the existence of inspection procedures cannot in any way relieve the fencers of responsibility for infractions of the rules.

B. *Organization of inspection*

The Central Office of the FIE or the Directoire Technique (or in their absence the Organizing Committee) may assign one or more special delegates to inspect the weapons and other equipment and clothing of the fencers.

This procedure is mandatory for the official competitions of the FIE, where the inspection must always be supervised by the members of the Commission on Electrical Scoring and Equipment.

18   The items of equipment which have been thus inspected will be labeled with a distinctive mark; a fencer may not, under pain of the penalties set forth below, use an item of equipment that does not bear this mark of inspection.

Besides the inspection procedures mentioned previously, the Director of a bout may at any time, on their own authority or at the request of a fencer or a team captain, either proceed to make an inspection, or verify the inspection procedures already taken, or perform or have performed new inspection procedures.

In any case, before each bout and at each change of weapon, the Director will check the insulation of the wires inside the guard and the strength of the point spring in electric weapons.

19   Before the beginning of each pool, each team match, and each bout in direct elimination, the Director, under the supervision of a member of the Directoire Technique or of a qualified delegate, will assemble the fencers in order to verify:

—that in electric foil competition the metallic vest conforms to Article 216 with the fencer in the various positions: standing, on guard, and in the lunge.

—that each fencer is wearing, under the jacket, a regulation protective undergarment.

Sec. 3. *Non-regulation equipment*

21   Under whatever circumstances a fencer on the strip is found to be in possession of non-regulation or defective equipment, that equipment will be immediately confiscated and turned over to the experts on duty for examination.

A. *If preliminary inspection of equipment has been carried out:*

1. *When a fencer appears on the strip:*
—with a non-working weapon or body wire, or
—without a protective undergarment, or
—with a metallic vest that does not completely cover the valid surface, the Director will give the fencer a warning valid for that pool, that team match, or during the direct elimination bouts.

In case of repetition of one or another fault, the Director will impose one penalty touch for each offense.

2. *When in the course of a bout an irregularity is demonstrated that could have arisen from the fencing:*

Examples:
—metallic vest with holes on which valid touches do not register,
—body wire or weapon no longer working,
—spring pressure having become insufficient,
—travel of the point no longer correct,

the Director will impose neither warning nor penalty. Moreover, a valid touch that has been scored with a weapon that has thus become defective will be awarded.

Sec. 5. *General requirements for clothing and equipment*

27   1. The equipment and clothing of the fencer must assure the maximum protection compatible with the freedom of movement essential to fencing.

2. It must not, in any way, risk interfering with or injuring the opponent;

V. RULES OF PLAY

neither may it include any buckle or opening that might, except accidentally, catch the opponent's point and thus hold or deflect it. The jacket and its collar must be completely buttoned or closed.

3. All garments must be white. They must be made of sufficiently strong material and be in good condition.

The material used for equipment shall not present a slippery surface capable of making the point, the button, or an opponent's cut glance off. The judging of touches shall be facilitated as much as possible.

4. In foil the bottom of the jacket must overlap the trousers by at least 10 cm when the fencer is on guard.

In all weapons the wearing of a protective undergarment is mandatory. The jacket and the collar must be completely closed and buttoned.

Women's equipment, in addition, must include in the jacket a breast protector of metal or some other rigid material.

5. The trousers [knickers] must be fastened below the knees. If the fencer is wearing long trousers, the bottoms shall either be buttoned or fastened above the feet.

With knickers, the wearing of a pair of white stockings is mandatory. They must cover the leg entirely up to the knickers and be fastened so that they cannot fall down.

6. In all weapons the cuff of the glove must always entirely cover the lower half of the forearm of the fencer's sword arm, to prevent an opponent's blade from entering the sleeve of the jacket.

7. The mask must be formed of mesh wherein the openings between the wires are at most 2.1 millimeters and of which the wires are of a minimum diameter of 1 mm before tinning, which should be carried out by a hot process after the mesh has been shaped.

In foil, the mesh of the mask must be insulated inside and out.

The bib and trim must be white.

FENCING ["COMBAT"]

Sec. 1. *Manner of fencing*

28 Competitors fence in their own style and at their own risk and peril, on the sole condition that they observe the fundamental rules of fencing.

All fencing must, nevertheless, maintain a courteous and honest character. All violent actions (a fleché ending by jostling the opponent, disorderly play, abnormal displacements, any actions that the Director judges dangerous—for example, a running attack involving loss of balance, hits brutally delivered) are expressly prohibited.

The fencer on the strip must keep his/her mask on until the decision has been given by the Director.

Sec. 2. *Distinctness of the touch*
29   In foil every hit must arrive clearly and distinctly to be counted as a touch.

Sec. 3. *Manner of holding the weapon*
30   Defensive actions are performed exclusively by the guard and the blade, used either separately or together. In the absence of a special device or attachment, the fencer is free to hold the hilt as he/she pleases and may likewise, in the course of a bout, change the position of the hand. However, the weapon may not, permanently or temporarily, in an open or concealed manner, be transformed into a throwing weapon; it must be managed without the hand leaving the hilt, and, in the course of an offensive action, without sliding the hand along the hilt from front to rear.

The weapon is managed by one hand only; the fencer may not change hands until the end of a bout, unless given permission by the Director to do so because of injury to the hand or arm.

The use of the unarmed hand and arm is prohibited, both on offense and on defense. The penalty for a violation is annulment of a touch that may have been scored and the penalty of a touch, after a warning given in the course of the same pool, same team match, or the bouts by direct elimination.

In foil in the course of a bout, it is likewise prohibited to protect or cover the valid surface [target] with the unarmed hand or arm. The penalty for a violation is the annulment of a touch that might have been scored on an opponent by the fencer at fault, or the penalty of a touch, after a warning given in the course of the same bout.

During the fencing action, under no circumstances may the fencer's unarmed hand grasp any part of the electrical equipment. The sanction for a violation of this rule is a penalty touch after a warning given in the course of the same bout.

Sec. 4. *Putting on guard*
31   The fencer first called must place themself on the Director's right, except in the case of a bout between a right-hander and a left-hander, if the left-hander is called first. The Director must place each of the two competitors so that their forward foot is 2 meters from the middle line of the strip (i.e., behind the "on-guard" line).

Placement on guard at the beginning of a bout and all replacements on guard are always made in the middle of the width of the strip.

The guard position is assumed by the fencers on the Director's command "On guard." After which, the director asks "Are you ready?" Upon an affirmative reply, or in the absence of a negative reply, the Director gives the command to begin: "Fence."

V. RULES OF PLAY

In case the Director observes in the course of the bout that one of the fencers is using the unarmed hand or arm, he/she may ask for the assistance of two judges, as neutral as possible, who will be named by the Directoire Technique. These judges, located on either side of the strip, will each watch one fencer and indicate, by raising a hand or in response to the Director's question, any use of the unarmed hand or arm. The Director alone will decide the penalties to be imposed.

The Director may likewise have the two fencers change places, so that the one who commits this irregularity does not have their back toward him/her.

Sec. 5. *Beginning, stopping and restarting the bout*

1. As soon as the command "Fence" has been given, the competitors may begin offensive action. No action begun or completed before the command is counted.

2. The end of action is marked by the command "Halt," except for special cases that change the regular and normal conditions of fencing.

As soon as the command "Halt" has been given, a fencer may not begin a new action; only an action already under way remains valid. Everything which happens afterwards is completely invalid.

If one of the fencers stops before the command "Halt" and is touched, the touch is valid.

The command "Halt" is also given if the play of the fencers is dangerous, confused or contrary to the rules, if one of the fencers is disarmed, if one of the fencers leaves the strip completely, or if, in retreating, the fencer nears the spectators or judges.

3. After each touch awarded as valid, the fencers are put back on guard at the center of the strip. If the touch is not awarded, they are put back on guard in the positions they occupied when the bout was interrupted.

The fencers change sides

—outdoors, after each touch;

—indoors, after each bout in direct elimination; or, in bouts for several touches, after one of the fencers has received half of the maximum number of touches that can be received.

However, with an electrical scoring machine, the fencers do not change sides during the bout.

4. Except in unusual circumstances, the Director may not permit a fencer to leave the strip.

Sec. 6. *Fencing at close quarters* [infighting]

33   Fencing at close quarters is permitted as long as the fencers can use their weapons normally, and, in foil, as long as the Director can continue to follow the action ["phrase d'armes"].

Sec. 7. *Corps a corps*
34   The "Corps a corps" exists when the competitors are in bodily contact; in this case, the Director halts the bout.

Sec. 8. *Evasive actions, displacing the target, passing the opponent*
35   Displacements and evasive movements are permitted, even those in which the unarmed hand may come in contact with the ground.

However, displacements executed in order to retreat by turning the back on the opponent are prohibited; the sanction for this violation is a penalty touch, after a warning valid for the same bout.

Furthermore, turning the back on the opponent during the fencing action is prohibited. The sanction for this violation is the annulment of any touch scored after a warning valid for the bout.

In the course of a bout, when a fencer passes their opponent, the Director must immediately give the command "Halt" and put the fencers back on guard in the places they occupied before the passing action occurred.

When touches are made in the course of a passing action, the touch made immediately [on the pass] is valid, and a touch made after passing the opponent is annulled; but one made immediately, even by turning around, by the fencer who has been attacked, is valid.

When in the course of a bout a fencer who has made a fleché attack has a touch registered against him/her and yet continues to run beyond the end of the strip far enough to tear free the reel or reel wire, the touch received will not be annulled.

Sec. 9. *Ground gained or lost*
36   At the command "Halt," ground gained is held until a touch has been awarded. When they are put back on guard, the fencers must each retire an equal distance to reestablish fencing distance.

37   Howovor:

a) When the bout has been stopped because of a corps a corps, the fencers are replaced on guard so that the one who sustained the corps a corps is at the place previously occupied; the case is the same if the opponent has made a fleché attack, even without a corps a corps.

b) A replacement on guard may not have the effect of putting behind the warning line a fencer who was in front of it when the bout was stopped, if this fencer has not already been warned.

c) A replacement on guard may not cause loss of ground to a competitor who was behind the warning line when the bout was interrupted.

Sec. 10. *Crossing the boundaries of the strip*
a) Stopping the bout
38   When a competitor crosses one of the boundaries of the strip with

V. RULES OF PLAY

both feet, the Director must immediately call "halt" and annul everything which happened after the crossing of the boundary, except a touch received by the fencer who crossed the boundary, even if it was received after the crossing, provided it resulted from an immediate parry-riposte.

When one of the fencers leaves the strip, only the touch scored under these conditions by the fencer who stays on the strip can be awarded, even in the case of a double touch, with the exception, however, of the case set forth in Article 42.

b) Rear limits and warning lines

39   When a fencer's rear foot has reached their warning line for the last time, according to the rules proper to each weapon, the Director gives the command "Halt" and warns the fencer of the ground remaining before the rear limit of the strip will be crossed. This warning is repeated each time the fencer, after having regained the on-guard line with the forward foot, again reaches the warning line with the rear foot. The fencers are not warned at any other location on the strip.

40   The competitor who, after a warning, crosses—i.e., crosses with both feet—the rear limit of the strip, is declared touched. However, if the fencer crosses the rear limit without having been warned, he or she is put back on guard at the warning line.

41   The ground must be used as many times as is necessary to allow each fencer the benefit of the full regulation length for retreating, but they will be warned only when they reach the warning line for the last time.

42   If, after having crossed the rear limit, the fencer attacked parries and immediately ripostes ["tac-au-tac"] or makes a stop, or executes a stop with opposition, the touch thus scored is valid. This provision is not applicable to the fencer who crosses the rear limit of the strip for the last time.

c) Lateral boundaries

43   If a competitor crosses the lateral boundary of the strip with only one foot there is no penalty, but the Director must immediately give the command "Halt" and put the fencers back on guard on the strip.

The competitor who crosses one of the lateral boundaries with both feet is penalized. Upon the return on guard, the opponent will be advanced from the position held at the moment of the action by one meter, in foil; the fencer penalized must withdraw the same distance.

The competitor who is placed beyond the rear limit of the strip with both feet by this penalty is declared touched, provided that they had already been warned at the warning line.

The fencer who crosses one of the limits with both feet to avoid being touched—particularly in making a fleché—will be penalized one touch,

after a warning given in the course of the same bout.
d) Leaving the strip accidentally
44   The competitor who crosses one of the limits as a result of an "accident" (such as a collision) is not liable to any penalty.
Sec. 11. *Duration of the bout*
45   By duration of the bout is meant effective duration, that is, the sum of the periods between the commands "Fence" and "Halt," not counting time used for deliberations of the jury or for other interruptions.

The effective duration of a bout is:
—for one-touch épée: 5 minutes
—in all weapons, for 4 touches = 4 minutes
for 5 touches = 6 minutes
for 8 minutes = 10 minutes
for 10 touches = 12 minutes

46   One minute before the expiration of the time allowed for fencing, the timekeeper must rise and call out: "Minute," without stopping the clock; this action alerts the Director, who halts the bout and notifies the fencers that "approximately" one minute remains to fence.

The touch started at the moment of the Director's "Halt" remains valid.

In cases of a prolonged interruption of the bout during this last minute, the fencers may, upon coming back on guard, be informed of the time remaining to them for fencing.

At the expiration of the regulation time, the timekeeper must call "Halt" (or sound a signal)—which stops the bout, and even an action already started is not valid.

In case of a failure of the timekeeper or of the time clock, the Director must estimate the time remaining to fence.

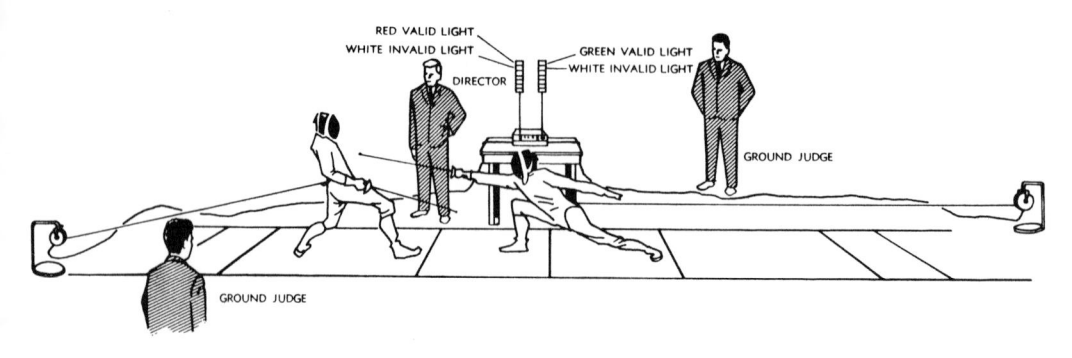

5.2 Electrical Fencing with Floor Judges

V. RULES OF PLAY

48 In the course of a bout, the Director may penalize by a warning, then by a touch, and then by exclusion from the competition, a fencer who improperly endeavors to create or prolong interruptions of the bout.

Sec. 12. *Accidents—indispositions—withdrawal of a fencer*

50 If a fencer is the victim of an accident duly verified by the physician on duty, the Director may allow a maximum of one 20-minute rest period to regain their condition to fence.

51 In case of an indisposition duly verified by the physician onduty, the Director may allow a fencer one 10-minute maximum rest period.

52 The Director, after consulting a physician on duty, may require the withdrawal of a fencer whose physical incapacity to continue is apparent.

THE DIRECTION OF A BOUT AND THE JUDGING OF TOUCHES

A. OFFICIALS

Sec. 1. the Director ["President"]

53 Every fencing bout is under the control of a Director who:

   a) Calls the roll of the fencers.

   b) Directs the bout.

   c) Inspects the equipment, including the insulation of wires, particularly on the inside of the guard.

   d) Supervises the assistants (judges, floor judges, timekeepers, scorekeepers, etc.).

   e) Maintains order.

   f) Penalizes offenses.

   g) Awards the touches.

Sec. 2. *The Jury: Judges and Floor Judges*

54 The Director accomplishes a mission either with the assistance of four judges or with the aid of an automatic touch signaling machine, with, as may be necessary in that case, the assistance of two judges watching for the correct use of the unarmed hand or arm or of the two floor judges.

Floor judges are required in case there is no metallic strip (*Fig. 5.2*).

The Director and the judges (or floor judges) compose the "Jury." For all bouts starting with the quarter-finals, the Director must be assisted by two judges, each watching one of the fencers with the responsibility for signaling any interference by the unarmed arm (in foil, either to deflect the opponent's weapon or to cover part of the valid surface).

Hand and floor judges must change sides at mid-point of the bout in foil so as not to be always judging the same fencer.

55   In accepting service on a jury, each of its members agrees on their honor to respect the rules and to enforce them, as well as to perform their duties with the most scrupulous impartiality and the most sustained attention.

Sec. 3. *Auxiliary personnel*

1. Scorekeepers and timekeepers

59   Whenever it is possible for them to do so, the organizers will appoint, on their own responsibility, scorekeepers who will be responsible for keeping the score sheet for the pool and the score boards, and a timekeeper who will be responsible for timing the duration of the bouts.

B. JUDGING BY A JURY

Sec. 1. *Duties of the Director*

61   the Director will be stationed at a distance from the strip that will permit him or her to follow the actions of the fencers thoroughly as they move up and down the strip.

Sec. 2. *Location of the jury (Fig. 5.3)*

62   On each side of the strip there are two judges, respectively to the right and left of the Director, and a little behind the fencers. The two judges on the Director's right watch the fencer on the Director's left, particularly to observe the materiality of touches that may be received by that fencer.

In similar fashion, the two judges on the Director's left watch the fencer on the Director's right, particularly to observe the materiality of touches that may be received by that fencer. (See, however 69/4.)

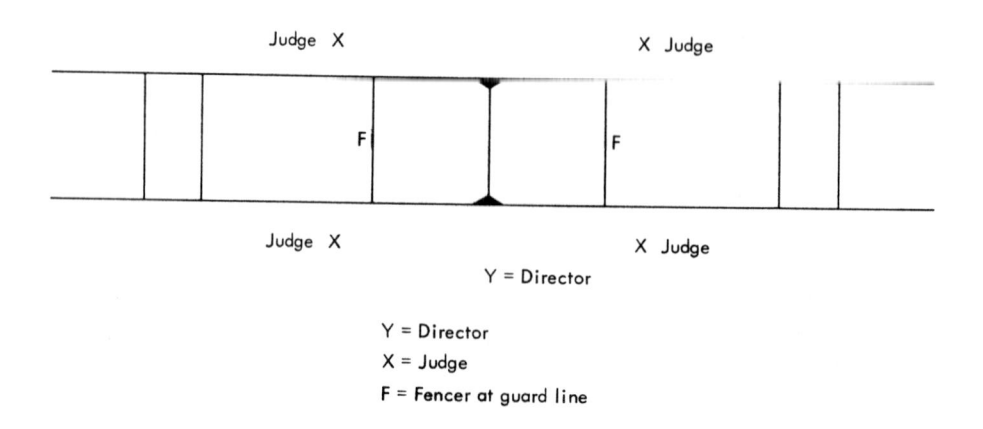

Judge X   X Judge

F   F

Judge X   X Judge

Y = Director

Y = Director
X = Judge
F = Fencer at guard line

5.3 The Jury

V. RULES OF PLAY

Sec. 3. *Judging*

a) Procedure

63 The Director, who alone is responsible for the direction of the bouts, gives the commands. However, another member of the jury may call "Halt," but only in case of an apparent or imminent accident. Similarly, the timekeeper stops the bout by calling "Halt" at the expiration of time.

64 As soon as a judge sees a material touch (valid or not) against the fencer, their hand must be raised to advise the Director.

65 All judging is carried out aloud and without the members of the jury leaving their places.

66 The jury is not bound by the acknowledgement of a touch by a fencer, even when properly made.

67 The jury first determines the materiality of the touch or touches. The Director alone then decides which fencer is touched, by applying the conventional rules for each weapon.

b) Materiality of the touch

68 Immediately upon stopping of the bout, the Director briefly analyzes the actions composing the last phrase d'armes before the "Halt" (this formality is not required in épée), and in the course of the analysis, asks the two judges watching the same fencer to learn if, if in their opinion, each of the actions thus analyzed has produced a touch against that fencer. The same is done with the other two judges for the other fencer (these formalities are mandatory in all three weapons).

The judges, upon being questioned, must reply in one of the following ways: "yes," "yes, but on invalid surface [off-target]," "no," or "I abstain." The Director votes last.

69 The Director adds the votes elicited on each side: the opinion of each judge counts as one vote and the Director's own opinion as a vote and a half, with abstentions not being counted:

1. If both judges on one side agree in a definite opinion (either both "yes" or both "no," or both "yes, but on invalid surface"), their judgment prevails.

2. If one of the judges has a definite opinion and the other abstains, the Director alone can decide, since that vote is preponderant. If the Director also abstains, the vote of the judge having a definite opinion prevails. prevails.

3. If the two judges have definite but contradictory opinions or if they both abstain, the Director may decide; if he or she also abstains, the touch is considered doubtful (see Para. 5 below).

4. In case of a double abstention, the Director may, as an exception to the usual practice, ask the other two judges if they were better located to

see the touch—for example, when a fencer who has run past an opponent on a fleché has had a riposte aimed at their back.

5. A touch of doubtful materiality is never counted to the disadvantage of the fencer who may have received it; but, on the other hand, any touch made subsequently or simultaneously in the same phrase d'armes by the fencer who has benefited from this doubt must also be annulled; as for a touch subsequently made by the fencer who had made the doubtful touch, it is necessary to distinguish:

I. —If the new touch (remise, redoublement, or riposte) is made by the fencer who had made the doubtful touch, without any intervening touch by the opponent, this new touch must be awarded.

II. —But if the doubt as to the place where the touch arrived (one "yes" and one "yes, but off-target"), no further touch in that phrase d'armes can be awarded.

III. —The situation is the same if, between the doubtful touch and the new touch made by the same fencer, the opponent has also made a touch that has been annulled as doubtful.

c. Validity or priority of the touch

70   After the decision of the jury on the materiality of the touch, the Director, acting alone and by application of the rules conventional for each weapon, decides which fencer must be declared touched, or if no valid touch is to be awarded.

C. JUDGING WITH A SCORING MACHINE

Sec. 1. *Direction of the bout*

71   1. The bout is under the control of the Director who must be stationed to be able to follow the fencing while also being able to watch for the light signals.

2. At the beginning of each bout, the Director must inspect the weapons, uniforms and equipment of the fencers.

As for the weapons, and at each change of weapon, the Director, using a special weight, will verify the strength of the spring in the point and will check on the insulation of the wires within the guard.

THE CONVENTIONS OF FENCING WITH THE FOIL

A. METHOD OF MAKING TOUCHES

219   The foil is a thrusting weapon only. An offensive action with this weapon must therefore be made with the point, and only with the point. Every thrust with the point must arrive cleanly and plainly to be counted as a touch.

V. RULES OF PLAY

B. VALID SURFACE [TARGET]

Sec. 1. *Limitation of the valid surface*

220   In foil, only those touches that reach a surface classified as valid [the target] are counted.

The valid surface, in both women's and men's foil, excludes the limbs and the head. It is limited to the trunk of the body, reaching at the top to the upper edge of the collar to a height of six centimeters above the top of the collar bones (clavicles); at the side, it reaches the seams of the sleeves, which should pass over the top of the humerus; at the bottom, it follows a line that passes horizontally across the back at the level of the top of the hip bones, and from there proceeds in front by straight lines to the junction of the groin.

221   The bib of the mask is not part of the target.

Sec. 2. *Extention of the valid surface*

222   Touches arriving on a part of the body classified as invalid are counted as valid when, by an abnormal position, the fencer has substituted this invalid surface for a valid surface. The Director may question the judges (hand judges), but must alone decide whether the touch is valid or not.

Sec. 3. *Invalid surface*

223   A touch that arrives on an invalid surface (whether directly or as the result of a parry) is not counted as a valid touch, but stops the phrase d'armes and thus annuls all subsequent touches.

C. CORPS A CORPS AND FLECHÉS

224   In foil, whenever a fencer intentionally or systematically causes the corps a corps (even with neither brutality nor violence), one touch must be penalized—after a warning given in the course of the same bout.

D. NUMBER OF TOUCHES—DURATION OF THE BOUT

225   In foil, bouts are for 5 touches for men and for women, with a duration of 6 minutes per bout; in direct elimination, two bouts of 5 or 4 touches, with a deciding bout if necessary, or bouts for a specified number of touches.

226   When the time runs out before the bout is decided:

   a) if one of the competitors has received more touches than the other, there is added to that score the number of touches necessary to arrive at the maximum, and the same number is also added to the score of the other fencer;

   b) if the two fencers are tied, they are both regarded as having received the maximum number of touches, less one; and they fence without limit of time for the last touch. They are put back on guard at the positions they occupied when the bout was interrupted.

E. JUDGING TOUCHES IN FOIL

227 Foil competitions are normally judged with the aid of an electrical scoring machine. For other competitions, the organizers are obliged to announce in advance if the competition will be judged by a jury.

I. MATERIALITY OF THE TOUCH

Sec. 1. *With a jury*
 (See 64.)

Sec. 2. *With a scoring machine*

228 1. For judging the materiality of the touch, the indication of the scoring machine alone is the determinant. In any case, the Director may not declare a fencer touched unless the machine has properly registered the touch (except in case of penalties provided in the rules).

229 In using the scoring machine, note that:

  a) if the two signals on the same side (both white and colored) are lit, the invalid touch preceded the valid touch;

  b) otherwise, the machine does not indicate whether there was any priority in time between two or more touches that it registers at the same time.

230 2. The Director will disregard signals resulting from thrusts:

  —started before the command "Fence" or after the "Halt."

  —touching the ground (outside the metallic strip or when there is none), or touching any object whatsoever other than the opponent or their equipment (see 73f).

  The fencer who intentionally causes a touch signal by putting the point on any surface whatsoever other than the opponent, shall be penalized one touch—after a warning given in the course of the same pool, the same team match, or during the bouts by direct elimination.

  It is forbidden for a fencer to put an uninsulated part of their weapon in contact with their metallic vest with the intention of blocking the operation of the machine and thus avoiding being touched.

  The penalty for this violation is the annulment of a touch that may have been scored by the fencer who causes the blocking of the machine and a warning valid for the whole pool, the same team match, or the bouts in direct elimination.

  At the first repetition, annulment of a touch that may have been scored and the awarding of a touch as a penalty."

  In case of a second repetition, exclusion from the competition.

231 3. The Director, on the other hand, must take into account possible defects in the scoring equipment, particularly:

  a) Must annul the touch just awarded as the result of the appearance

V. RULES OF PLAY 105

of a valid touch signal (colored lamp), if established, by tests carried out under careful supervision, and before any effective resumption of the bout and without anything having been changed in the equipment in use:

—either that a "valid" touch signal is produced against the fencer declared touched without there actually being a valid touch;

—or that an invalid touch made by the fencer declared touched is not registered by the machine;

—or that a valid touch made by the fencer declared touched produces no signal, either valid or invalid;

—or that touch signals produced by the fencer declared touched do not remain fixed on the machine.

b) On the other hand, when the Director has determined that one fencer's touch had the priority [right of way], there is no ground for annulling that touch if tests then show that a valid touch made by the fencer declared touched is registered as invalid or that the latter's weapon gives a permanent invalid signal.

c) If a fencer's equipment does not conform to the specifications, there is no ground for annulment in case a valid signal is produced by a touch on the invalid surface.

4. The Director must also apply the following rules:

a) only the last touch preceding the establishment of a defect can be annulled;

b) the fencer who, without being asked by the Director, has made modifications in, or has changed, equiment before the Director has given a decision, loses all righ to annulment of a touch (see 71/13);

c) if there has been an effective resumption of the bout, a fencer may not claim the annulment of a touch awarded against him or her before the said resumption;

d) the localization of a defect found in the equipment (including the fencers' own equipment) is of no consequence for this possible annulment;

e) it is not necessary that the defect found should repeat itself at every test; but it is necessary that it have been positively observed at least once in the course of tests made by or under the supervision of the Director;

f) the sole fact that the fencer declared touched has broken their blade is not sufficient to annul that touch;

g) the Director must be especially alert for touches that are not signalled, or abnormally signalled, by the machine. In case of repetition of these defects, the Director must call for the member of the Commission on Electrical Scoring and Equipment who is present, or for the technical expert on duty, in order to determine whether the equipment conforms to the rules.

The Director must watch that nothing is changed, either in the fencers' equipment, or in the whole of the electrical equipment, before the inspection by the expert.

5. In all cases in which the verification has been made impossible as the result of accident, the touch will be regarded as "doubtful" (see 69/5).

6. If signals appear on the apparatus simultaneously from both sides and the Director cannot establish the priority [right of way] with certainty, the fencers must be put back on guard.

7. In application of the general rule (see 32), even if no signal has been registered, the Director must halt the bout as soon as the action becomes confused and it is no longer possible to analyze the phrase d'armes.

8. The Director must also watch the condition of the metallic strip. The Director will not permit the bout to be started or to be continued if the metallic strip has holes capable of interfering with the registration of touches. (The organizers shall make provision for the rapid repair or replacement of metallic strips.)

II. VALIDITY OR PRIORITY OF THE TOUCH [RIGHT OF WAY]

Sec. 1. *Preliminary note*

232   Whatever means the Director has used to reach a decision on the materiality of the touch (with the assistance of a jury or by aid of a scoring machine), it is then his/her responsibility *alone* to decide on the subject of the validity or priority [right of way] of the touch, by applying the following principles which are the conventions proper to foil fencing.

Sec. 2. *Observance of the phrase d'armes (fencing phrase)*

a) Every attack, that is, every initial offensive action, correctly executed, must be parried or completely avoided and the phrase must be followed through, that is, coordinated.

To judge the correctness of an attack, the following points must be considered:

1. The simple attack, direct or indirect, is correctly executed when the extending of the arm with the point threatening the valid surface precedes the beginning of the lunge or fleché.

2. The composite attack is correctly executed when the arm extends in the presentation of the first feint, with the point threatening the valid surface, without withdrawal of the arm during the execution of the successive movements of the attack and the beginning of the lunge or fleché.

3. The attack by advance-lunge or advance-fleché is correctly executed when the extending of the arm precedes the end of the advance and the beginning of the lunge or fleché.

4. The attack, simple or composite, executed with a bent arm is a badly

V. RULES OF PLAY

executed attack and exposes the attacker to the beginning of an offensive or defensive action (see 12) of the opponent.

To judge the priority (right-of-way) of an attack in the analysis of the phrase d'armes, the following points must be considered:

5. If the attack begins when the opponent is not "in line," that is, with the arm extended and the point threatening the valid surface, it may be made either by a direct thrust, or by a disengagement, or by a coupé, or even be preceded by a beat or by effective feints obliging the opponent to parry.

6. If the attack begins when the opponent is "in line," that is, with the arm extended and the point threatening the valid surface, the attacker must, as a preliminary, deflect the opposing weapon.

7. If, in searching for the opposing blade to deflect it, the attacker does not find the blade (derobement), the right-of-way passes to the opponent.

8. If the attack, the advance, or the feints are executed with the arms bent, the right-of-way passes to the opponent.

234 b) The parry gives the right of way to the riposte; the simple riposte may be direct or indirect, but to annul any subsequent action of the attacker, it must be executed immediately, without indecision or delay.

235 c) In a composite attack, if the opponent finds the blade on one of the feints, he or she has the right to riposte.

236 d) In composite attacks, the opponent has the right to make a stop; but to be valid the stop must precede the conclusion of the attack by a period of fencing time, i.e., the stop must touch before the attacker has commenced the last movement of the conclusion of the attack.

Sec. 3. *Judging*

237 In applying these fundamental conventions of the foil, the Director must judge as follows:

Whenever, in a phrase d'armes, the fencers are both touched simultaneously, there has been either a *simultaneous action* or a *double touch*.

The former is the result of simultaneous conception and execution of the attack by both fencers; in this case, the touches given are annulled for both fencers, even if one of them has touched an invalid surface.

The double touch, on the contrary, is the result of a faulty action on the part of one of the fencers.

Consequently, if there is not a period of fencing time between the two touches:

1. *The fencer attacked is alone counted as touched—*

a) if he or she makes a stop into a simple attack;

b) if, instead of parrying, the fencer attempts to avoid being touched, and fails;

c) if, after a successful parry, the fencer pauses for a moment—which gives the opponent the right to resume an attack (redoublement, remise, or reprise);

d) if, on a composite attack, the fencer makes a stop without having the advantage of a period of fencing time;

e) if, being in line (arm extended and point threatening a valid surface), after a beat or a taking of the blade which deflects the weapon, the fencer attacks or replaces the blade in line instead of parrying a direct thrust made by the attacker.

2. *The attacker alone is counted as touched—*

a) if the fencer starts their attack when the opponent is in line (arm extended and point threatening a valid surface) without deflecting the opposing blade;

b) if the fencer attempts to find the blade and fails (because of a derobement or trompement) and still continues the attack;

c) if, in a composite attack, in the course of which the fencer's opponent finds the blade, he or she continues the attack while the opponent immediately ripostes;

d) if, in a composite attack, the fencer hesitates for a moment during which the opponent delivers a stop thrust, yet he or she continues the attack;

e) if, in a composite attack, the fencer is hit by a stop made with the advantage of a period of fencing time before the conclusion;

f) if the fencer touches by remise, redoublement, or reprise, after a parry by the opponent which is followed by an immediate simple riposte executed in one period of fencing time and without withdrawl of the arm.

3. *The fencers are replaced on guard,* every time that the Director cannot decide clearly which side is at fault in a double touch.

One of the most difficult cases to decide occurs when there is a stop and there is doubt as to whether it had a sufficient time advantage over the conclusion of a composite attack. In general, in this case, the double touch is the result of simultaneous faults by the fencers, which fact justifies the replacement on guard. (The fault of the attacker lies in indecision, slowness or inefficient feints; the fault of the fencer attacked lies in delay or slowness in making the stop.)

Scoring

The duty of the scorekeeper shall be to record the scores against fencers after they have been awarded by the Director.

All touches in fencing are recorded against the fencer receiving them. Therefore, the fencer receiving the greater number of touches is the loser.

V. RULES OF PLAY

The scorer announces the score after the hit has been awarded, and at the conclusion of the bout enters the scores on the score board. The scorekeeper announces the names of the next competitors who are to go on the piste and those who will follow them.

The majority of fencing competitions are round-robin. The term round-robin implies that all competitors compete against each other. Since the number of contestants can be quite large, the fencers are often placed in smaller groups called pools. Each fencer within a pool competes against all others in that pool. The fencer winning the greatest number of bouts is declared the champion of the pool. Should there be a tie for first place, it is fenced off. This is called a barrage. The remaining places are determined by indicators. A total of all touches scored against one's opponents minus all those received by a fencer determines the place. The result is the greater the difference in the above two components, the better the score.

It is customary in championship tournaments for 50% or more of the fencers to advance to the next round from the preliminary pools.

| WEAPON | FOIL | POOL | III | DATE | 12-3 |

Place	Name		1	2	3	4	5	6	7	8	W	L
	KEENAN, B.	1				IIII/L						I
	DICKMAN, M.	2			IIII/L							I
	EVANS, M.	3		O/W							I	
	CRAMER, N.	4	II/W								I	
		5										
		6										
		7										
		8										

4 FENCERS 6 BOUTS	5 FENCERS 10 BOUTS		6 FENCERS 15 BOUTS		7 FENCERS 21 BOUTS		8 FENCERS 28 BOUTS			
1-4	1-2	1-3	1-4	6-4	1-4	5-1	3-5	2-3	8-7	7-5	2-6
2-3	3-4	2-5	2-5	1-2	2-5	4-3	1-6	1-5	4-1	3-6	3-5
1-3	5-1	4-1	3-6	3-4	3-6	6-2	2-4	7-4	5-2	2-8	1-7
2-4	2-3	3-5	5-1	5-6	7-1	5-7	7-3	6-8	8-3	5-4	4-6
3-4	5-4	4-2	4-2	2-3	5-4	3-1	6-5	1-2	6-7	6-1	8-5
1-2			3-1	1-6	2-3	4-6	1-2	3-4	4-2	3-7	7-2
			6-2	4-5	6-7	7-2	4-7	5-6	8-1	4-8	1-3
			5-3								

5.4 Fencing Scoresheet

The sample fencing score sheet shows the procedure for keeping score (see Fig. 5.4). The order of bouts for four fencers determines the competition. The first bout was between Keenan, No. 1, and Cramer, No. 4. A line was drawn through the box in the fourth column on the number 1 line and through number one column on the number 4 line. Each hit scored against fencer No. 4 was recorded by a hash mark in the top half of that individual's scoring box, and the same procedure was followed for fencer No. 1. At the end of the bout, a *W* was recorded in the bottom half of the winner's scoring box and an *L* in the loser's. The wins and losses for each fencer are recorded in the win-loss column at the right following each bout. The foregoing scoring procedure is followed for each bout. As the fencers are called to the piste, the scorer should place a line through their numbers in the order of bouts so scoring is kept up to date.

The Timer

The timer has as their specific duty the keeping of actual fencing time. When the Director gives the command to fence, the timekeeper starts the bout clock and keeps it running until the Director calls halt. The timer continues to start and stop the bout clock with the Director's commands throughout the bout. The timer also notifies the Director, who in turn warns the fencers, when only one minute of fencing time remains in the bout.

Evaluation Questions

1. What are the two names often used for the field of play?
2. What are the basic differences between men's and women's foil bouts?
3. What constitutes a good hit?
4. What are the four responses a judge in the jury system may use?
5. Who is the official who awards touches?
6. How are touches scored?
7. What do fencers do when the score is tied at the end of a bout?
8. What is fencing time?
9. What type of competition is used most frequently for fencing tournaments?

CHAPTER SIX

Etiquette and Safety

Throughout history an elaborate system of etiquette has developed and continually been associated with sword play, particularly the sport of fencing. Many of the courtesies practiced today are a direct carryover from the era of dueling. The practice of etiquette in fencing today has led to the sport being one of the more stringent regarding the conduct of the participant. When one looks at the era of dueling, one finds that the upper class was primarily interested in the art of fencing. This class was composed predominantly of noblemen totally committed to proper, genteel behavior. The sport of fencing has always attracted a very high caliber individual. Displays of poor sportsmanship and rudeness are not tolerated in any type of competition. The competitor is expected to act with restraint, control, and poise.

When one is involved in sparring in free play with an opponent, it is considered proper to acknowledge each hit received. One seldom sees or hears fencers arguing over the validity of a touch. When this is observed, someone immediately steps in and reminds the fencers of the rules of the sport. A fencer is expected to possess the qualities of neatness, politeness, modesty, and at the same time have a very confident composure. The fencer is expected to be mannerly in discussion with other fencers and courteous when making introductions to the opponent prior to a competition. It is also considered very proper for a new competitor to introduce themself to the members of the jury and/or the director prior to a bout. A fencer is expected to salute the opponent and the officials prior to a bout. Many fencers make an optional salute to the audience. During formal competition when a discussion or deliberation is being carried on by the officials, the fencer is to remain in a position of attention and is not to interject comments, argue, or talk back to the officials during the deliberation. Any display of rudeness or attempt to influence the judges will bring an immediate reprimand.

Fencers are not to hit after the buzzer sounds in electrical competition nor after a halt is called. Any persistence will result in a reprimand. During the actual competition, if one's opponent has scored a good touch, it is often considered a positive acknowledgement of that skillful hit to salute one's opponent after the touch has been awarded by the director. This is not mandatory but, again, a gentle display of courtesy. In jury competition, fencers often shake hands as they pass when directed by the official to change ends of the strip.

Following the decision of a touch, a fencer may politely ask for an explanation of the action and the decision. He/she may not in any way question or imply rudely that the decision was wrong or that it had been handled improperly.

At the end of a bout, the fencers should remain masked until the final decision regarding the outcome of the bout has been announced. At that time, each may remove their mask, step forward, and shake hands. Upon leaving the strip the fencer should thank the officials whose efforts have made the bout possible, and leave the strip with a posture of composure and self control. Many times because of the intenseness of the competition, tempers flare and people become emotional, but fencers should retain their composure at all times. Such behavior as storming from the strip or throwing helmet and foil against the wall will result in a reprimand.

Safety

The sport of fencing has been, and continues to be, a very safe sport if people follow a few basic safety principles. Good equipment is a necessity and should include proper clothing, glove, mask, and foil. When one is considering an investment in personal fencing equipment, corners should never be cut to save a few dollars. It has been proven consistently that good quality equipment will far outlast a cheaper quality. Better quality equipment also insures a much better fit and requires less time for care and repair. With proper maintenance, equipment can be expected to last over a period of years.

All items of equipment should be worn properly. In order to cool slightly, a fencer will often open the jacket at the neck. Before facing an opponent,the jacket should be completely closed about the neck, the helmet and bib should be in place, and the glove worn on the foil hand.

Regular laundering of fencing clothing will add to its life. Perspiration, which accumulates in a jacket, will eventually weaken the thread and cause the jacket to rot if not laundered frequently. Gloves should be allowed to dry thoroughly and should be cleaned frequently. Perspiration does cause the leather to deteriorate. Allowing the glove to dry in such a position

VI. ETIQUETTE AND SAFETY

that air can circulate in and around it will add to its life. The mask should be inspected periodically for holes or breaks on the mesh, since a blade could hit a weakened area and penetrate the mask.

Foil blades should be examined periodically and sanded so that any steel splinters are removed. The tips or buttons should be examined frequently to make certain they are in place and that the blunted end of the foil is not cutting through the protective tip. Blades do break occasionally and should be immediately discarded. There should never be any attempt to use a broken blade.

In examining the equipment used for electrical fencing competition, one should make certain that the metallic vests are cleaned frequently and that there are no holes or breaks in the metal mesh of the fabric. If a hole or a break in the mesh is discovered, the vest should be removed from competition. Body cords should be examined periodically to ensure there are no breaks in the wires. Electrical foils should be examined prior to competition to ensure that they meet competitive specifications.

Often in jest people will spar freely without protective equipment on. One should never face another opponent with blades in a position to fence without wearing a mask, jacket, and gloves. Many accidents have happened even when fencers never intended to get close enough to contact their opponent.

By practicing the above etiquette and safety recommendations, one can enjoy the sport of fencing with all its color and flourish for a great many years.

Evaluation Questions

1. Should one acknowledge a hit received during free play?
2. Whom should a fencer salute prior to the beginning of a bout?
3. Can fencers ask the director for a description of the blade action preceding a touch?
4. When can a fencer remove his mask while on the piste?
5. What kind of care should be given to one's fencing clothing and equipment?

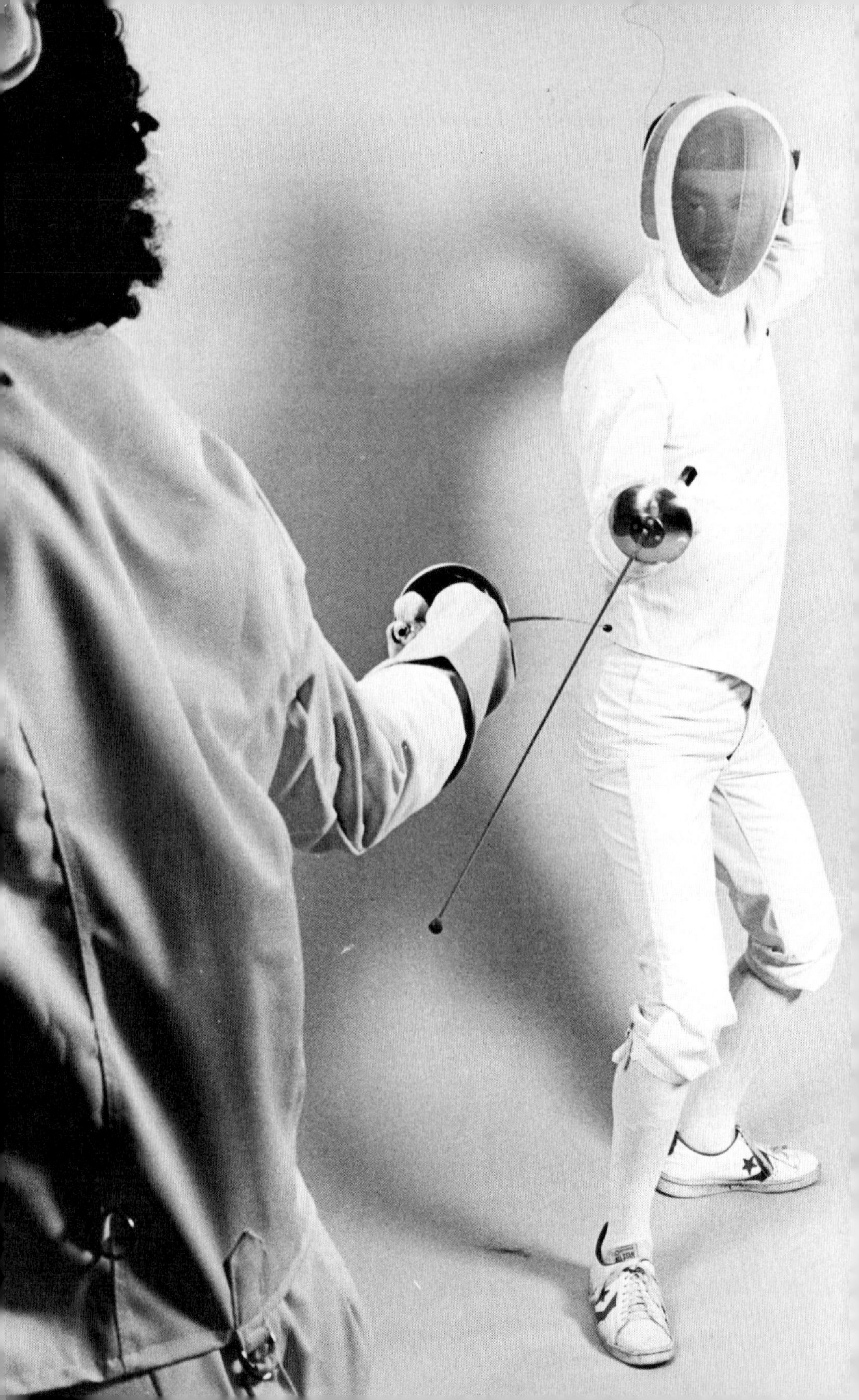

CHAPTER SEVEN

Bouting Strategy

Once a fencer has mastered the fundamentals of the foil, he/she is ready to move on to competitive experiences. Coupled with the acquisition of skills, one must attain certain analytical abilities to test, observe, and interpret the actions and reactions of one's opponent. Upon completion of the testing with feints or authentic attacks and observation of the opponent's reaction and movement patterns, the fencer's interpretation will determine the strategy to use when combating opponents.

The ability to analyze one's opponent thoroughly, coupled with the implementation of correspondingly effective offensive and defensive strategies, are two of the major components of a fencing champion.

Beginning the Bout

Prior to the beginning of the bout, one should appear confident and ready for combat. During the approach to the piste and the salute, one should act poised and experienced. As the bout begins, one should test the opponent with feint attacks to determine whether or not there are any habitual blade actions and if the opponent is telegraphing intended movements.

For example, the opponent may continually use one parry when another might be more effective. As one tests for habitual patterns, one can also determine the reaction time and speed of the opponent and their finesse with the blade. The use of the invitation, the intentional opening of any line to entice the opponent into making an attack, will assist one in determining the reach of the opponent. If the opponent has a long and controlled lunge, one will need to exercise caution with regard to a fencing distance and may need to retreat a step with defensive blade actions. However, as soon as the defense is complete, one should immediately attempt to regain the ground lost during the retreat.

Knowing Your Opponent

The following are a few suggestions for implementing strategies in opposing certain fencing styles. Fencers should be reminded that these are only a few suggested tactics, and that successful application of skills and tactics is dependent on the creativity in one's mind and one's ability to think.

Opponent's Foil Arm Is Carried in a Position of Extension. Should the opponent fence with the foil arm continually extended, one should employ attacks on the blade, which take and control the opponent's blade.
- Beat
- Bind
- Bind with fleche
- Glide
- Press
- Envelopment

Opponent Has a High Position of Guard. If the opponent continually carries their foil in a high position of guard, the following actions could be employed.
- Attack to the low line.
- Feint to the low line and, upon the opponent's reaction to the feint, attack to the high line.
- Glide.
- Bind from a high line to a low line.
- Beat up and attack low.

Opponent Has a Low Position of Guard. Should the opponent continually carry his/her foil in a low position, one should attempt the following attacks.
- Attack to the high line.
- Feint to the high line and attack to the low line on the opponent's reaction.
- Beat down on the opponent's blade and attack high.
- Bind from a low line to a high line.
- Glide.
- Coupé to high line.

Opponent Is Tall. The following tactics are suggested when fencing a taller opponent.
- Be extremely cautious when attempting to gain ground.
- Employ second intention attacks.
- Beat.
- Bind.
- Envelopment.
- Lower your own guard stance and close your high line, making it more difficult to get to your own target.
- Straight attacks to the low line.

VII. BOUTING STRATEGY

Opponent Is Small. When one is confronted with an opponent who is small, the following strategies could be employed.
- Immediately test their reaction time.
- Carefully keep distance.
- Use stop-thrusts whenever possible.
- Close low line.

Opponent Does Not React to Feints. It is common to encounter an opponent who does not react to feints. This can be quite frustrating to an attacking fencer. The tendency is to continue attempting feints with the hope of finally evoking a response from the opponent, but this type of fencing can become very fatiguing. One should attempt the following actions.
- Invite the opponent.
- Execute simple attacks with great speed.

Opponent Has Strong Blade Action. If one's opponent has very strong blade action and attempts to dominate the blade, use the following techniques.
- Make the blade unavailable to the opponent.
- Continually vary the position of guard.
- Utilize counter-parries so all defensive movements will have definite strength.
- Allow the opponent to initiate the attack.
- Do not attempt to engage the blade.

Opponent Continually Stop-Thrusts. When one's opponent continually utilizes the stop-thrust, employ the following tactics.
- Concentrate on simple attacks.
- Bind.
- Glide.
- Envelopment.
- Attack with opposition.
- Feint attack, then bind.

Opponent Has Weak Parries. When confronted with an opponent who has weak parries, try the following blade actions.
- Feint attack and then remise.
- Compound attacks.

Opponent Has a Slow Riposte. When fencing with one who has a slow riposte, the following skills are suggested.
- Feint attack and then remise.
- Feint attack and then reprise.

Opponent Continually Offers an Invitation. If you are confronted with an opponent who continually offers an invitation, employ the following strategies.
- Use 1-2 attack.
- Use 1-2-3 attack.
- Simple attack with great speed.
- Advance, extend, and threaten until he/she regains the guard position.
- Feint to determine if the opponent consistently uses a specific parry. Once it has been determined that he/she does, plan attacks to deceive that parry.

Opponent Is Left-Handed. Many times a right-handed fencer is defeated in competition because he/she is matched with a left-handed opponent. This is usually due to the fencer's lack of knowledge and experience in combating the left-handed opponent. A common remark often heard in relation to this is, "Everything seems to be backwards." By keeping a few key points in mind, the right-handed fencer need not fear the left-handed opponent.

As play begins, gradually force the left-handed opponent to the left side of the piste and make an effort to keep them there for the remainder of the bout. Generally speaking, parries that protect the outside lines are the weaker ones, while parries that protect the inside lines are the stronger ones. The right-handed fencer should:
- Insist on the engagement in their own fourth, which will force the left-handed opponent to engage in sixth.
- Plan the attacks so they end in the outside line.
- Feint to the low outside line but land in the high outside line.

If one is a left-handed fencer competing against a right-handed fencer, attempt the following tactics.

As play begins, attempt to force the right-handed fencer to the right side of the piste and make a continued effort to keep him/her there throughout the bout. The left-handed fencer should:
- Insist on the engagement in their own inside lines, which will force the right-handed opponent to engage in the outside lines.
- Plan attacks so they end in the outside line.
- Feint to the low outside line but land in the high outside line.

Generally speaking, left-handed fencers do not have many problems adjusting to right-handed fencers. Left-handed fencers are in a minority and have had to practice against right-handed fencers during most of their practice sessions. Many of the problems encountered by the right-handed fencer combating the left-handed fencer can be diminished through practice. Since experience in the situation is extremely important, the right-handed fencer should fence with a left-handed opponent whenever the opportunity presents itself.

Skill alone does not make a champion. A fencer must learn to analyze their opponent. After this is learned, one can confidently match a more experienced fencer who has developed specific movement patterns.

Evaluation Questions

1. *Which parries are considered to be the weaker ones?*
2. *Why is it important to know how to analyze one's opponent?*
3. *Why does the beginning left-handed fencer have an advantage over the beginning right-handed fencer?*
4. *When should a fencer test their opponent? Why?*
5. *Name other possible habits one could encounter in addition to those mentioned. How can these additional habits be handled?*

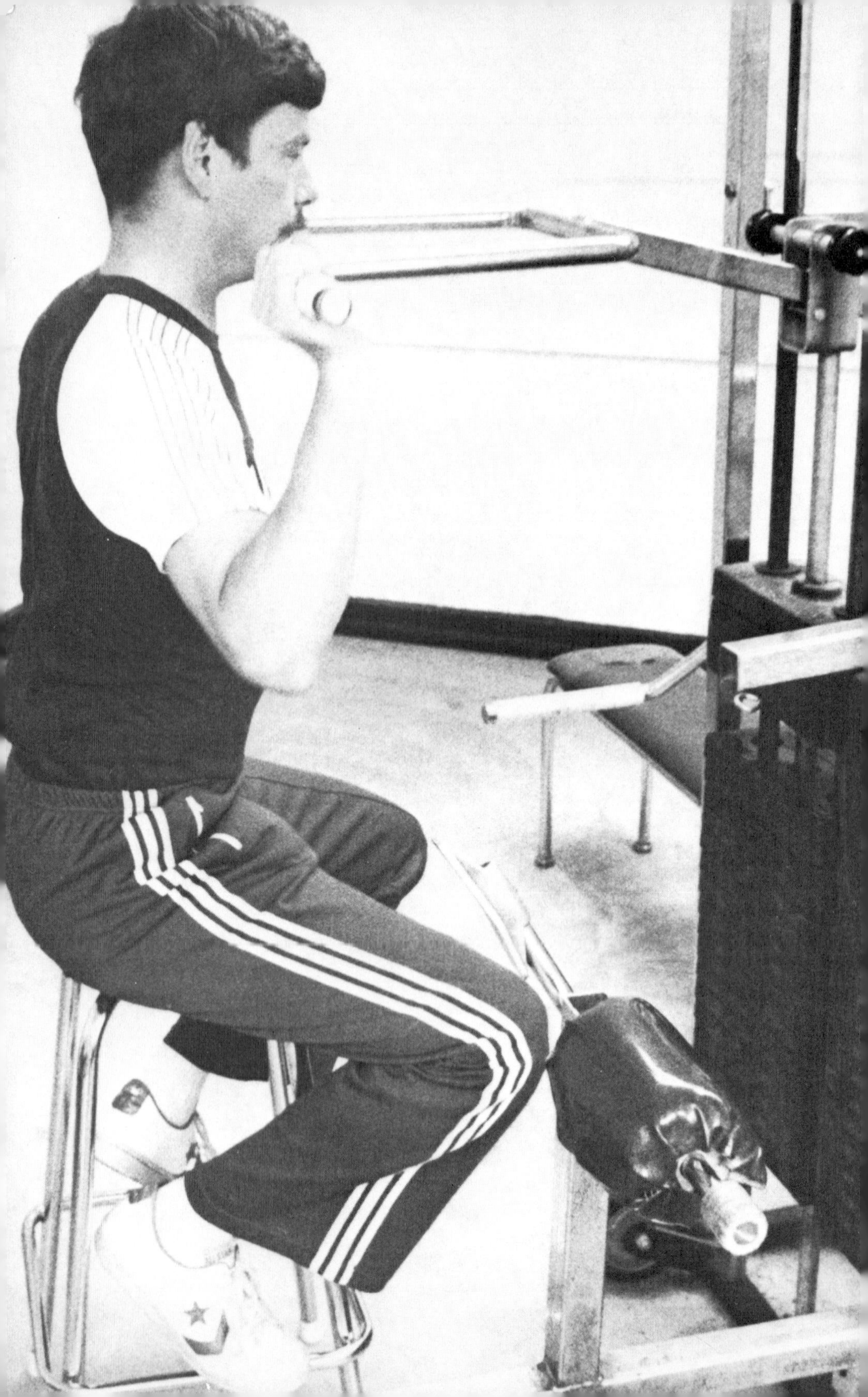

CHAPTER EIGHT

Conditioning

In all athletic competition, sound conditioning plays a very important role. It differentiates the athlete who excells from one who merely participates. Proper conditioning in the areas of muscular strength, muscular endurance, cardiovascular, and cardiorespiratory endurance and flexibility are all necessary considerations for the competitive fencer. Muscular strength is defined as the ability to lift or move a certain amount of weight. Muscular endurance is the ability to repeat a specific strength task a number of times. Cardiovascular and cardiorespiratory endurance is the ability to perform specific tasks and to recover efficiently and effectively in a relatively short period of time. Flexibility is the ability to move the body or certain areas of the body through a full range of motion without inducing pain or injury to that area of the body.

the Warm-Up

The value of a proper warm-up period before vigorous exercise has been supported many times in current research literature. One of the primary functions of this warm-up period is to reduce or minimize the possibility of injury. It is recommended that one start with some light jogging in order to increase the heart rate. This should be followed by some stretching exercises to aid in joint and muscle flexibility. When doing flexibility work, one should start with slow static stretching and avoid ballistic movements. Research has shown that static stretching allows greater relaxation of opposing muscle groups and results in greater improvement of flexibility. There is less chance of injury to the muscle or ligamentous tissues. Ballistic movements produce a rapid and intense reflex and can cause overstretching and possible injury. The following are some suggested flexibility exercises.

In the body hang (Fig. 8.1), the individual flexes forward at the hip allowing the upper torso to hang with the hands toward the toes. The knee should be in a position of easy extention. The weight of the upper torso should be allowed to just hang, so that it slowly stretches the hamstrings and increases flexibility in that area. This position should be held for ap-

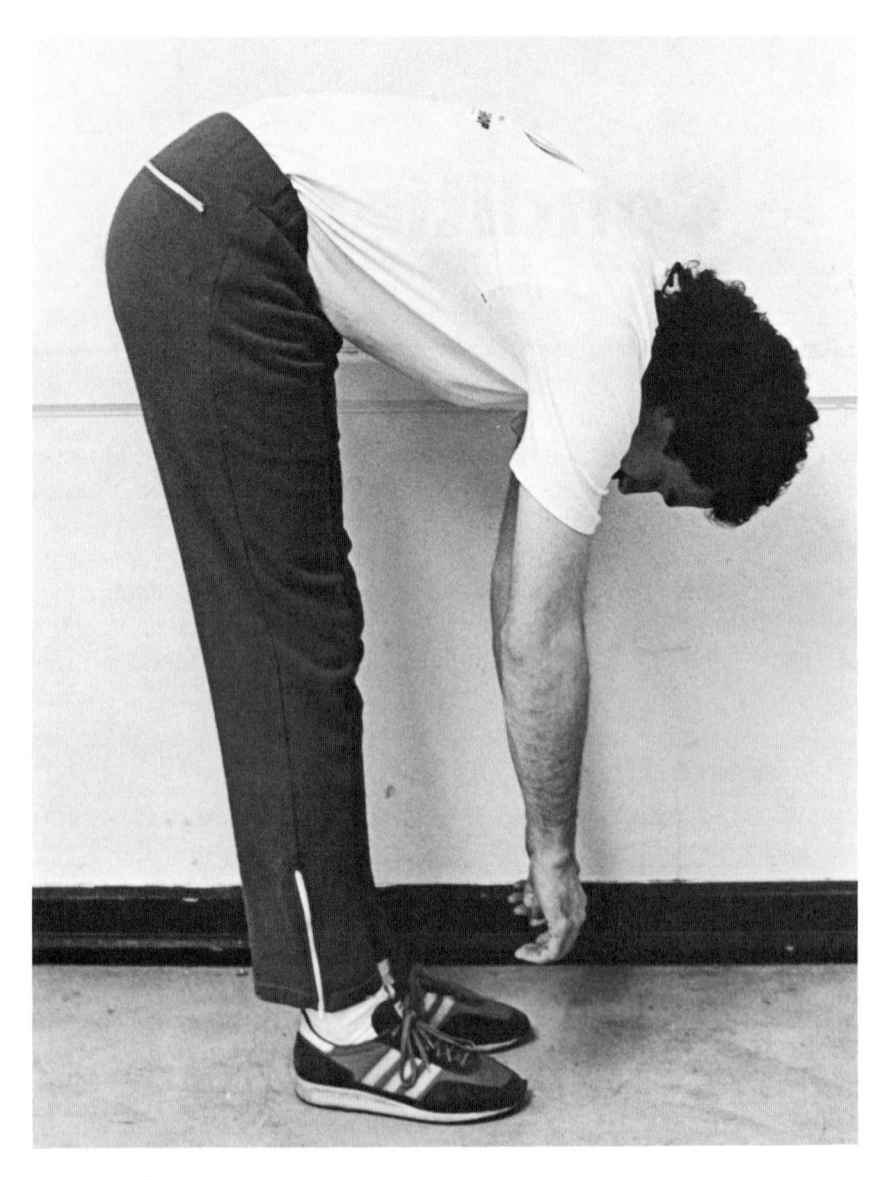

8.1 Body Hang

proximately 10 to 15 seconds. One should remember not to bounce down in order to touch the floor in this exercise. As flexibility increases, the fencer should be able to shorten the distance between palms and the floor without undue pain in the hamstrings. This is a gradual process that cannot be accomplished overnight.

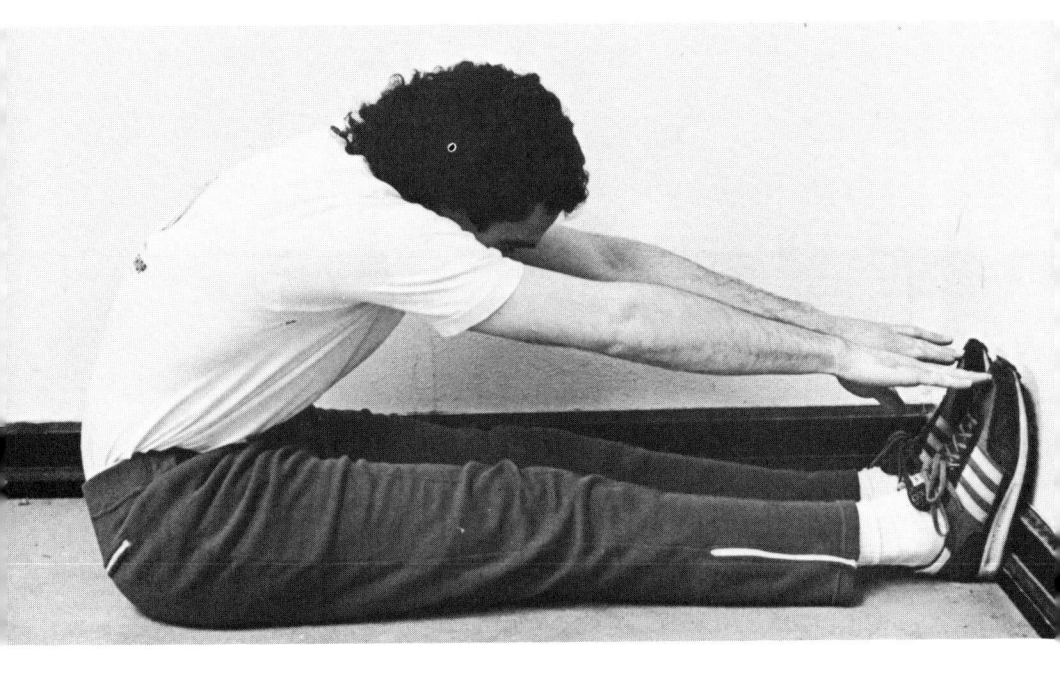

8.2 Touching Toes

8.3 Hurdler's Stretch

Assume a sitting position on the floor, legs extended, and bend forward to touch the toes with the hands. This position should be held for a count of 10 seconds and then relaxed (*Fig. 8.2*). One should not attempt a bouncing or ballistic type action in this position.

Another exercise that is excellent for increasing flexibility in the front and back of the thigh, groin, hamstrings, and back extensors is the "hurdler's stretch" (*Fig. 8.3*). With one leg flexed behind and the other in a

8.4 Straddle Stretch

position of extension, stretch toward the leading leg, grasp the foot, and hold to a count of 10 seconds. The leg positions are then alternated and the same count is repeated.

The lunge stretch is an excellent exercise for stretching the hamstrings, the aductors of the legs, the gastrocnemious and quadriceps. Assume the lunge position and allow the knee of the forward foot to go as far in front of the toe as possible so that the fencer is as low to the floor as possible. After holding that position to a count of eight, both feet are simultaneously pivoted one quarter turn in the opposite direction and the same exercise is repeated.

Another exercise that is good for flexibility and the low back extensors is the straddle stretch. Sit on the floor with legs spread apart and flex forward at the hips, allowing the elbows to touch the floor (*Fig. 8.4.*). Hold this position for approximately 10 seconds, then relax. Again, caution should be exercised to prevent ballistic movements.

Another flexibility exercise, which is useful in stretching the muscles and ligaments of the pelvic girdle, is called the Billig stretch (*Fig. 8.5*). The individual should stand with feet together and a side about 18 inches away from the wall. The right hand and forearm are placed against the wall at shoulder level. The hips are moved as close to the wall as possible and held for a count of ten. One should take care that hip rotation does not occur.

The above are just a few of the suggested flexibility exercises that should be practiced for a period of fifteen to twenty minutes prior to practice

VIII. CONDITIONING 125

8.5 Billig Stretch

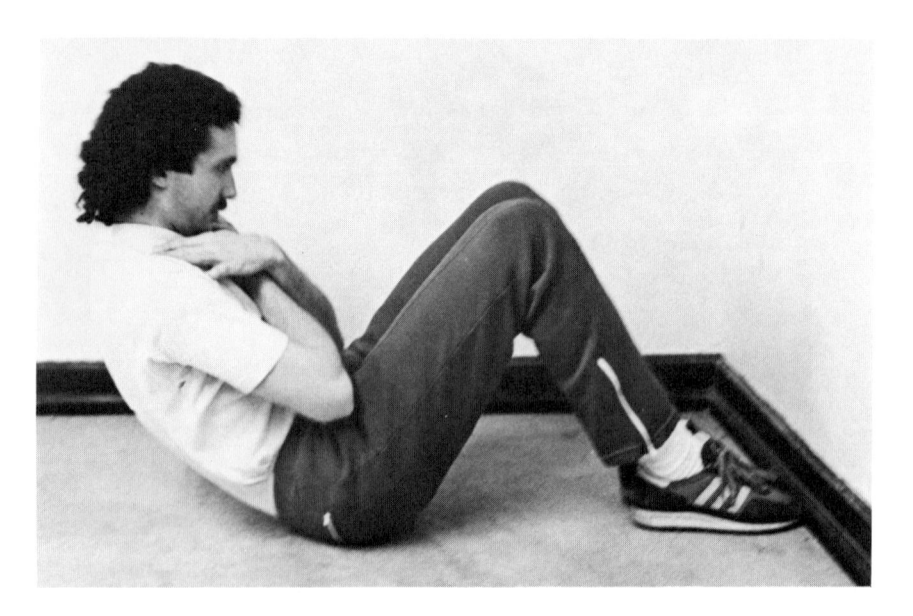

8.6 Curl Up

or competition. The fencer will then be better prepared for the vigorous exercise to follow.

The following are suggested vigorous strength exercises associated with fencing movements that might be incorporated into a conditioning program to insure that the fencer has the strength to endure a full day's competition.

The curl up is a form of the sit up. Sit on the floor with knees bent at approximately a 45 degree angle. Cross the arms over the chest and curl up to an upright position (*Fig. 8.6*). The number of repetitions should be gradually increased. The purpose of this exercise is to increase the strength in the abdominal wall.

Research has stated that deep knee bends can be hazardous to the athlete due to the intentional and continual stretching of the ligamentous structure. Strength in the legs is of vital importance to a fencer so it is suggested that knee bends be done with only enough flexion in the knee to allow the buttocks to rest on the edge of a chair, and then the exerciser returns to a standing position (*Fig. 8.7a and b*). In order to increase leg strength, the exercise can be done with the addition of free weights held above the shoulder to increase the strength of the muscles of the legs, lower and upper back. The number of repetitions should be gradually increased.

VIII. CONDITIONING 127

8.7a Knee Bends

Leg strength plus cardiovascular and cardiorespiratory conditioning can be gained by running stairs. To prepare for the sport of fencing, it is suggested that the athlete take the steps two or three at a time (*Fig. 8.8*). Walk down, however, because the constant jarring to the knee from body weight landing on the step can be injurious.

If your school or organization is fortunate enough to have a Universal Gym, the following exercises should be incorporated into a conditioning program. The amount of weight selected by the fencer should be determined by that which can be moved between eight and twelve repetitions. If

8.7b Knee Bends

8.8 Running Stairs

VIII. CONDITIONING

8.9 Bench Press

the fencer is unable to complete eight repetitions, too much weight is being attempted. If the athlete can readily move the amount more than twelve repetitions, the load is too light. Since the amount of weight lifted will vary, individual fencers should test each station in the conditioning program.

The bench press (*Fig. 8.9*). is an excellent exercise for the chest, shoulders, and the back of the upper arms. The individual lies flat on the bench with the knees bent. The hands are placed on the grips and the arms are extended and then slowly flexed back to the starting position.

The latissimus pull (*Fig. 8.10*) will strengthen the forearms, back and upper chest. One should start in a kneeling position and grasp the bar with the arms extended. The bar should be pulled down to the base of the neck and then slowly returned to the starting position. The upper torso should be kept straight throughout each repetition.

The shoulder press (*Fig. 8.11*) will strengthen the upper arms, back, and shoulder girdle. The individual sits on a stool directly under the bar,

8.10 Latissimus Pull

VIII. CONDITIONING

8.11 Shoulder Press

8.12 *Lateral Flexion*

VIII. CONDITIONING 133

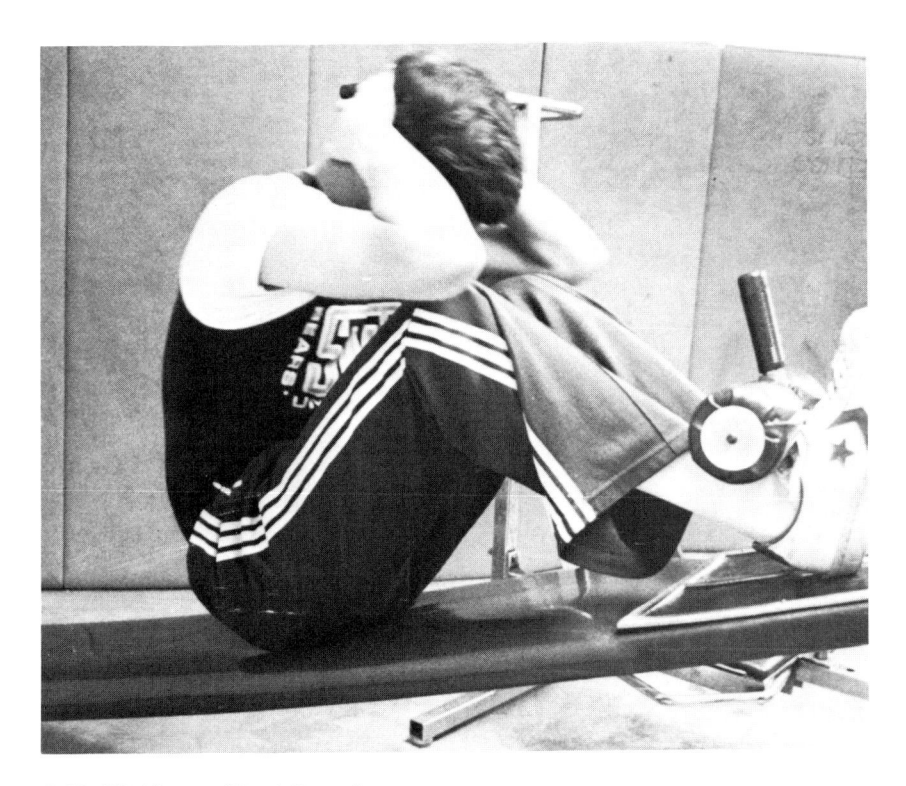

8.13 Sit Up on Slant Board

places his hands on the bar, slowly extends the arms above the head and then gradually flexes back to the original starting position.

The lateral flexion (*Fig. 8.12*) will increase strength in the lateral antigravity muscles of the hip and lumbar spine and the arm. Care should be taken so that hip flexion does not occur. Grasp the bar and pull sideways, then slowly return to the starting position.

Sit ups on a slant board (*Fig. 8.13*) place additional stress on the abdominal wall and also increase the range of work. The knees should be flexed and the individual sits up and slowly returns to starting position.

The leg press (*Fig. 8.14*) strengthens the buttocks, lower back and the thighs. The individual assumes a sitting position, hands at the sides, and slowly extends the legs. The legs are then flexed slowly to the starting position.

The leg curl (*Fig. 8.15*) strengthens the back of the upper legs, the gluteals, and hamstrings. Lie face down, legs extended, with the back of the heels against the bar. The feet should be lifted upward until they are over or touching the buttocks and then slowly returned to the starting position.

8.14 Leg Press

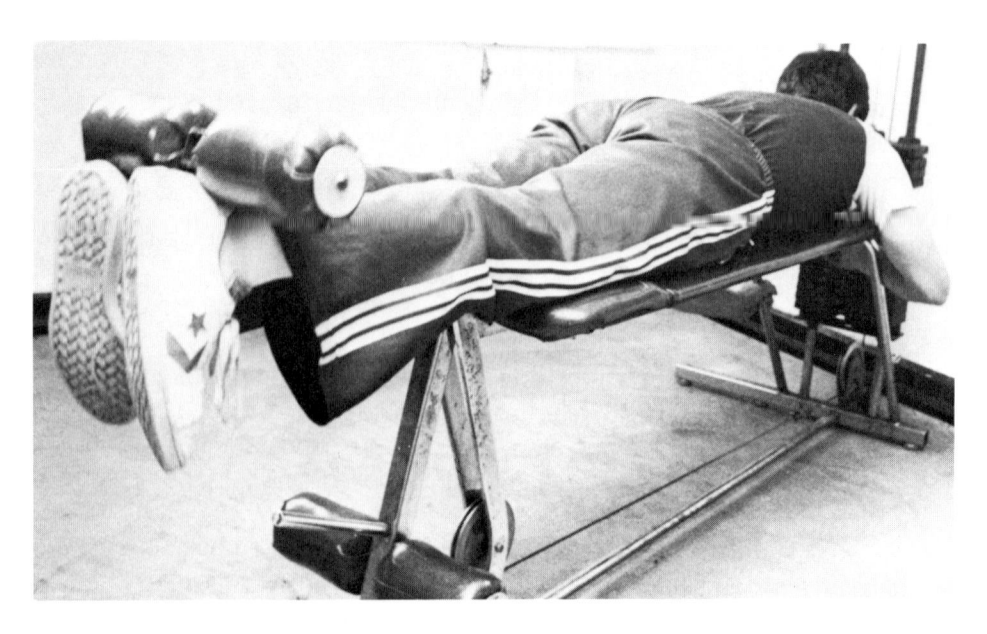

8.15 Leg Curl

Evaluation Questions

1. What is the difference between muscle strength and muscle endurance?
2. Why is a warm-up period important?
3. Which muscle groups are most affected by the bench press?
4. Why is cardiovascular and cardiorespiratory efficiency necessary for fencing?
5. How does flexibility fit into the fencer's total conditioning program?

CHAPTER NINE

Terminology

ABDUCTION A movement away from the mid-line of the body.

ABSENCE OF THE BLADE A fencing phase in which the blades of the opponents are not touching.

ABSTAIN The response a judge may use if he/she is unable to see whether or not the point landed.

ACTION ON THE BLADE Any movement in which a fencer effects a change in the opponent's blade by contacting it.

ADDUCTION A movement to or toward the mid-line of the body.

ADVANCE A forward stepping movement toward one's opponent.

ADVANCE-LUNGE (Pattinando) A quick advance step followed by a speedy lunge.

AMATEUR FENCERS LEAGUE OF AMERICA (AFLA) The former governing body of amateur fencing in the United States.

APPEL (call) A signal used by a fencer to display his/her wishes to stop a bout without danger of being hit. The appel involves stamping the forward foot quickly twice and then standing up backing away from the opponent very rapidly.

ATTACK Blade action, either compound or simple in nature, in which an attempt is made to hit the opponent's valid target area.

ATTACK ON THE BLADE An offensive action such as the press, beat, bind, or glide that removes the opponent's blade from line in order that the line be open for an attack.

BALLESTRA A jump toward one's opponent followed quickly by a lunge.

BARRAGE A fence-off of a tie between two or more competitors for first place.

BEAT A sharp rap with one's blade against the opponent's blade for the specific purpose of opening a line for an attack.

BELL GUARD The bell-shaped portion of the weapon between the blade and the handle, which protects the fencer's hand.

BIND An attack which, through continual contact of the opponent's blade, carries from a high line diagonally to a low line or vice versa.

BLADE That portion of the weapon from the button to the guard.

BODY CORD The insulated wire worn by a fencer which connects the foil to the floor reel and then to the scoring machine in electrical fencing.

BOUT Competition between two fencers.

BROKEN TIME A temporary alteration in the normal tempo of a bout.

BUTTON The covering placed over the blunted tip of the blade.

CADENCE The rhythm in which a phase of movements is made.

CALL (appel) A signal to convey to an opponent one's desire to stop a bout without danger of being hit. It is done by quickly stamping the forward foot twice, standing up and backing away from one's opponent very rapidly.

CHANGE OF ENGAGEMENT The movement of the blade from one line of engagement into another line of engagement.

CLOSING Two fencers in combat so close that neither can effectively or safely use their weapon.

CLOSING A LINE A defensive movement which involves automatically moving the guard of the foil position to close a line when an opponent engages in that line.

COMPOUND ATTACK An offensive blade action of two or more movements with the specific purpose of opening a line for attack.

CORPS-A-CORPS Two fencers body-to-body, bell guard-to-bell guard, a position which prevents normal fencing action.

COUNTER Describing a circle around the opponent's blade.

COUNTER-ATTACK A stop thrust or attack which takes time from the attacking fencer by touching before the final action of the original attacker begins.

COUNTER-PARRY A circular parry which is executed by parrying to the side directly opposite the one in which the attack was initiated.

COUNTER-RIPOSTE An offensive action which follows immediately the parrying of a riposte.

COUPE (cut-over) A simple attack which requires the foil blade to move up and over the tip of the opponent's blade to score in another line.

CUTTING THE LINE An over-reaction by a fencer while executing a

IX. TERMINOLOGY

parry which involves binding the opponent's blade from one line to another.

CUTTING WEAPON A weapon with which touches are made with the cutting edge of the blade rather than with the point.

DEROBEMENT A deceiving action executed with an extended arm which evades the opponent's attempt to beat or take the blade.

DEVELOPMENT A form of mobility involving a thrust of the foil arm followed immediately by a lunge.

DIRECT An attack, parry, or riposte taken in the line of original engagement.

DIRECTOR (president) The official who presides over a bout.

DISARMAMENT A strong blade action which causes the opponent to lose their blade.

DISENGAGE (cut-under) Leaving one line of engagement and moving into another by passing one's blade under the opponent's blade and scoring in another line.

DISTANCE The effective bouting space between two fencers in combat.

DOUBLE A compound attack which feints a disengage and deceives an opponent's counter-parry.

DOUBLE DISENGAGE An action which deceives the opponent's attempt to parry with two consecutive disengages.

DOUBLE TOUCH Both fencers hit each other simultaneously. Neither fencer has had the advantage of a clear right of way.

ENGAGEMENT The contact resulting when opposing blades cross.

ENVELOPMENT An attack which contacts and carries the opponent's blade in a complete circle and lands in the line of its original engagement.

ÉPÉE A thrusting weapon, heavier than the foil, which has as its target the entire body; used in competition by both men and women.

FALSE ATTACK An offensive ruse designed to elicit a specific response from one's opponent.

FEINT A subtle blade movement designed to lure the opponent into making a defensive response to a certain line. This feint is nearly always followed by an attack to another open line.

FENCING The art of offense and defense with a sword.

FENCING MEASURE The working distance for safe and effective sword play between two fencers in combat.

FENCE-OFF (barrage) A competition between two or more fencers to determine first place.

FENCING TIME The length of time necessary to complete one fencing action. This time may vary according to the skill and the pace of the fencers involved in the bout.

FEDERATION INTERNATIONALE D'ESCRIME (FIE) The official international governing body of fencing.

FIELD OF PLAY That area which contains regulation piste or strip.

FINGER PLAY The manual dexterity one utilizes in controlling the foil.

FLECHÉ (arrow) An attack made by running toward and past the opponent, with an attempt to touch the opponent before or while passing.

FOIBLE The weaker and more flexible portion of the blade nearest the tip.

FOIL A light, thrusting weapon; its target is the opponent's torso and is used in competition by both men and women.

FORTE The stronger and more rigid portion of the blade nearest the bell guard.

FOUL TOUCH A touch on the off-target area of a fencer.

GAINING GROUND Advancing toward one's opponent, forcing them to retreat on the piste.

GLIDE An attack along the opponent's blade in which the attacking fencer controls the weaker section of the opponent's blade with the stronger portion of their own blade.

GLOVE (gauntlet) Protective covering made of leather and/or canvas which is worn on the foil hand.

GRIP That portion of the handle on which a fencer positions the foil hand.

GROUNDING The electrical fencing circuitry which eliminates the registering of touches which score the blade, the bell guard, and the fencing piste.

GUARD POSITION The position of readiness that is basic to all mobility in fencing.

HELMET (mask) A sturdy, one-piece head, face, and neck covering with wire mesh front enabling the fencer to have complete visibility.

HIGH LINES The lines of attack and defense designated as those above the fencer's foil hand. These include both the outside and inside lines.

HIT An attack that lands and sticks on the valid or invalid target area of a fencer.

IX. TERMINOLOGY

INDIRECT An attack, parry, or riposte taken in a line other than that of the original engagement.

IN LINE The point of the attacking blade is one of the lines of attack and is threatening the valid target of the opponent.

IN QUARTATA A defensive movement in which the defending fencer side-steps or dodges an opponent's attack by backing away and turning one quarter turn toward the side.

INSIDE LINES The lines of attack and defense which are defined as those on the palm side of the fencer's target area. The inside lines include both the high and the low.

INSUFFICIENT PARRY A defensive action with the blade that merely caresses the attacking blade and is not strong enough to deflect the blade and prevent it from scoring.

INVALID TOUCH A hit that lands on the parts of the fencer's body and equipment that are considered off-target.

INVITATION The intentional opening of any line in an effort to entice one's opponent into attacking.

JUDGE A member of the jury who has the specific purpose of watching for hits and assisting the director.

JURY A team of officials, composed of four judges and one director, whose specific duty is to referee a bout.

LINES The four general areas of the target: high inside, high outside, low inside, and low outside.

LOSING GROUND Being forced to retreat on the piste when attacked by one's opponent.

LOW LINES The lines of attack and defense designated as those below the fencer's foil hand. These include both the inside and outside lines.

LUNGE An extension of the guard position made after an offensive blade action in order for one to reach the opponent's target.

MANIPULATORS The thumb and index finger of the foil hand.

MASK (helmet) A sturdy, one-piece head, face, and neck covering with wire mesh front allowing a fencer complete visibility.

MATCH Fencing competition between two teams.

MEET A fencing tournament.

METALLIC VEST A lamé jacket worn over the traditional fencing jacket and used exclusively in electrical fencing competition. The lamé jacket covers only the valid target area and allows for completion of the circuitry to register a valid touch with the electrical fencing apparatus.

MOBILITY Fencing movements utilized to gain or lose ground during fencing competition and more specifically to enable a fencer to reach an opponent when attacking.

NATIONAL COLLEGIATE ATHLETIC ASSOCIATION (NCAA) Provides guidelines for intercollegiate competition.

NATIONAL FENCING COACHES ASSOCIATION OF AMERICA (NFCAA) National organization for fencing coaches.

NATIONAL INTERCOLLEGIATE FENCING ASSOCIATION (NIFA) An organization for intercollegiate fencers.

NATIONAL INTERCOLLEGIATE WOMEN'S FENCING ASSOCIATION (NIWFA) An organization for intercollegiate women fencers.

OFF-TARGET HIT A hit that lands outside the valid target area.

ON GUARD The position of readiness basic to all fencing mobility.

ONE-TWO A compound attack consisting of a feint disengage and deception of the opponent's parry. This is often used as an advancing attack.

ONE-TWO-THREE A compound attack consisting of a feint disengage, disengage, and deception of the opponent's parries. This is often used as an advancing attack.

OPPOSITION The use of continual pressure as a means of controlling the opponent's blade either during an attack or riposte.

ORTHOPEDIC GRIP The grip of a handle designed with the specific purpose of fitting one's hand.

OUTSIDE LINES The lines of attack and defense designated as those on the dorsal or back side of the foil hand. The outside lines include both the high and low lines.

PARRY The defensive action on the opponent's attacking blade, used to deflect it and thereby prevent it from landing on a valid surface.

PASSATA-SOTTO A ducking action by a defending fencer which moves his/her target area totally below the attacking blade of the opponent.

PATTINANDO (advance-lunge) A rapid advance followed by a speedy lunge in the form of an attack toward one's opponent.

PASSE The tip of the foil slides on or across the target and does not stick.

PHRASE D'ARMES A sequence of fencing action by one or both fencers during combat.

PISTE (strip) The regulation field of play used for fencing competition.

POINT The tip of the foil blade; used for scoring touches.

IX. TERMINOLOGY

POMMEL The metal part which fastens to the tongue of the blade. It has two purposes: holding all the parts of the foil in place, and serving as a counter-weight to the blade, thus making the foil a balanced weapon.

POOL A group of fencers competing against each other in order to qualify for the next round of competition.

PRELUDE TO AN ATTACK A movement of the blade that serves to open a line for an attack.

PRESIDENT (director) The individual who presides over a fencing bout.

PRESS An application of continual pressure against the opponent's blade with the specific purpose of opening a line for attack.

PRISE-DE-FER Taking the opponent's blade or binding it.

PRONATION A movement of the hand that involves the rotation of the palm inward and downward.

RECOVERY TO GUARD A movement either forward or backward from a lunge or half-lunge to regain the guard position.

REDOUBLEMENT The immediate second effort of an attack, done without withdrawing the arm. This effort is made in a new line because the initial line is still closed.

REMISE An immediate second effort of an attack, done without withdrawing the arm. This effort is made in the same line as the original attack.

RENEWED ATTACKS Attacks such as redoublement, remise, and reprise.

REPRISE A retaking of the attack after an initial attack fell short. It usually is associated with a recovery forward so the distance between the fencers can be covered on the retaking effort.

RETREAT A systematic backward movement involving stepping away from one's opponent.

RIGHT OF WAY The right to attack, which is gained by the fencer who initiates the action by extending the foil arm toward the opponent's target. The foil point must be threatening the target of the opponent in order to have right of way.

RIPOSTE A counter-attack made immediately following a successful parry of the opponent's attacking blade.

SABRE A cutting and thrusting weapon which has as its target the entire torso from the waist up, including the head and the arms. This weapon is used in competition by both men and women.

SALLE D'ARMES A facility specifically designed for fencing, such as a fencing room.

SALUTE A method of acknowledging one's opponent and the officials prior to the beginning of a bout.

SCORE (touch) A valid hit on target. Touches are scored against the fencer being touched. The fencer with the smallest number of touches at the end of a given period of time is declared the winner.

SECOND INTENTION ATTACK Fencing strategy with a specific purpose of using the first movement to draw the opponent into a response and then deceiving that response and scoring on the second movement. The attacking fencer intends to score on the second movement throughout the blade action.

SEEDING Ranking individual fencers within pools of competition according to their fencing ability.

SIMPLE ATTACK An attack consisting of one movement. Three simple attacks are: the straight thrust, the coupé, and the disengage.

SIMULTANEOUS ACTION Both fencers conceive and initiate an attack at the same time without either having the advantage of right-of-way.

STOP THRUST A counter-attack made during the opponent's attack at the time a hesitation or delay occurs in that attack. In order to count as a valid touch, the stop thrust must land before the opponent's final movement begins.

STRAIGHT ATTACK A simple direct thrust with no change of lines and usually combined with a lunge.

STRIP (piste) The regulation field of play used for fencing competition.

SUPINATION Rotation of the hand and palm, upward and outward.

TARGET That portion of the fencer's person on which valid hits can be scored. The target includes the torso of the body—the front, sides, and back from the waist to the neck. The arms are excluded.

TEMPO The timing or pacing of the movements of a fencer.

THRUST The rapid extension of the foil arm with the intention of scoring a touch.

THRUSTING WEAPON A weapon with which hits are scored by the point.

IX. TERMINOLOGY

TIME THRUST A counter-attack made into the opponent's blade serving as both a parry and riposte.

ULNAR FLEXION The wrist bends so the little finger side of the hand is near the forearm.

WARNING LINES Lines placed one meter from the end of the fencing piste. When a fencer retreats to a point where his/her foot is touching the warning line, a warning is given noting that he/she is approaching the end of the strip.

WRIST FLEXION The wrist bends so the palm side of the hand is near the forearm.

WRIST HYPEREXTENSION Wrist bends so the back side of the hand is near the forearm.

UNITED STATES FENCING ASSOCIATION (USFA) Formerly AFLA. The governing body for fencing in the United States.

Suggested Readings

Amateur Fencers League of America, Ind. *Fencing Rules,* 1974.

Amateur Fencers League of America, Inc. *supplement to the 1974 Rule Book.* Executive Secretary, Eleanor Turney, 601 Curtis Street, Albany, California 94706.

Anderson, Bob. *All About Fencing.* New York: Arco Publishing Co., 1970.

Angelo, Domenico and Henry. *The School of Fencing.* New York: Land's End Press, 1971; reprint of 1787 ed.

Barbasetti, Luigi. *The Art of the Foil.* New York: E.P. Dutton, 1932.

Bower, Muriel. *Fencing.* 3rd ed. Dubuque, Iowa: Wm. C. Brown Company, 1976.

Castello, Hugo, and Castello, James. *Fencing.* New York: The Ronald Press Co., 1962.

Castello, Julio Martinez. *The Theory and Practice of Fencing.* New York: Charles Scribner's Sons, 1933.

Crosnier, Roger. *Fencing with the Foil.* New York: The Ronald Press Co., 1951.

Garret, Maxwell R., and Heinecke, Mary F. *Fencing.* Boston: Allyn and Bacon, Inc., 1971.

Palffy-Alpar, Julius. *Sword and Masque.* Philadelphia: F.A. Davis Company, 1967.

Selberg, Charles A. *Foil.* Reading, Mass.: Addison-Wesley Publishing Co., 1976.

Simonian, Charles. *Fencing Fundamentals.* Columbus, Ohio: Charles E. Merrill Publishing Co., 1968.

United States Fencing Association, *Fencing Rules.* U.S.F.A., 1750 East Boulder Street, Colorado Springs, Co. 80909

About the Author

Nancy Curry received her B.S. and M.S. in Education at Emporia Kansas State College. She later obtained her doctoral degree in Physical Education at the University of Southern California.

Dr. Curry is the author and editor of several books and articles on a variety of sport-related subjects, including fencing. An active professional, she has been a member and held office in numerous sports, political and community based organizations. She has also done extensive lecturing and consultation at both the local and national level. In addition, she has been the head coach of successful fencing, field hockey and track teams at Iowa State University and Southwest Missouri State University. Dr. Curry is also the recipient of various special honors. Among these honors is her inclusion in the prestigious *World's Who's Who of Women in Education.*

Currently, Dr. Curry is a Professor of Physical Education at Southwest Missouri State University.

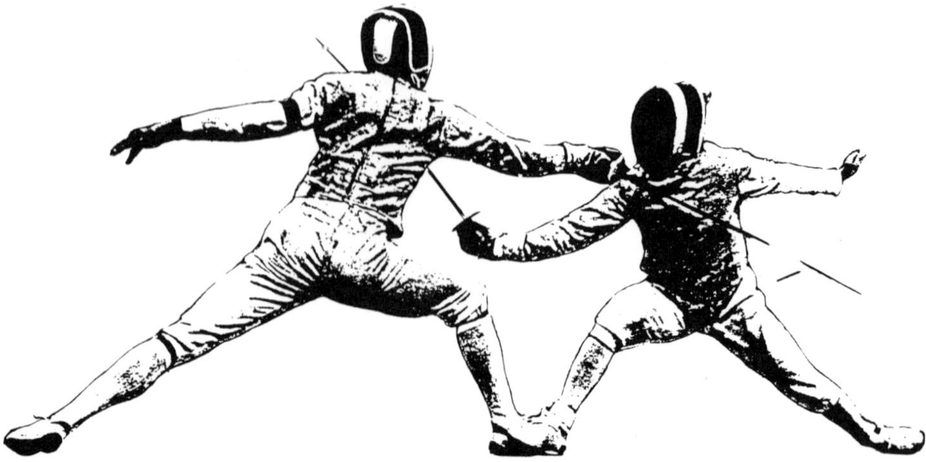